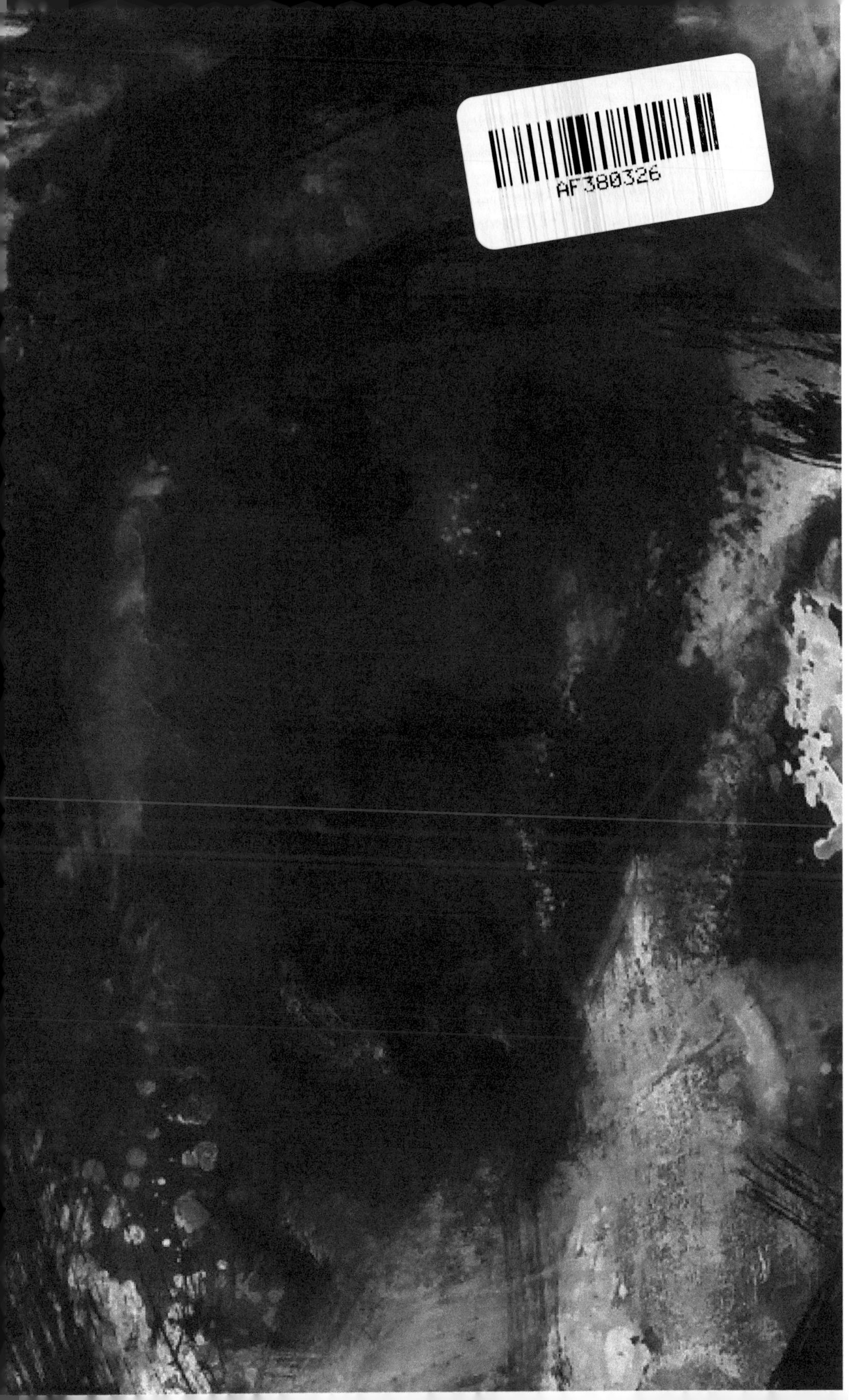
AF380326

Parson's Porch Books

Drawings of Jesus

ISBN: Softcover 978-1-946478-03-0

To order additional copies of this book, contact:

Parson's Porch Books

1-423-475-7308

www.parsonsporch.com

Parson's Porch Books is an imprint of Parson's Porch & Company (PP&C) in Cleveland, Tennessee. PP&C is an innovative company which supports people who live in poverty by allowing them to earn money by assisting in publishing books by noted authors, representing all genres. To help people in poverty, PP&C totaling depends on the generosity of its authors and partners.

Drawings of Jesus

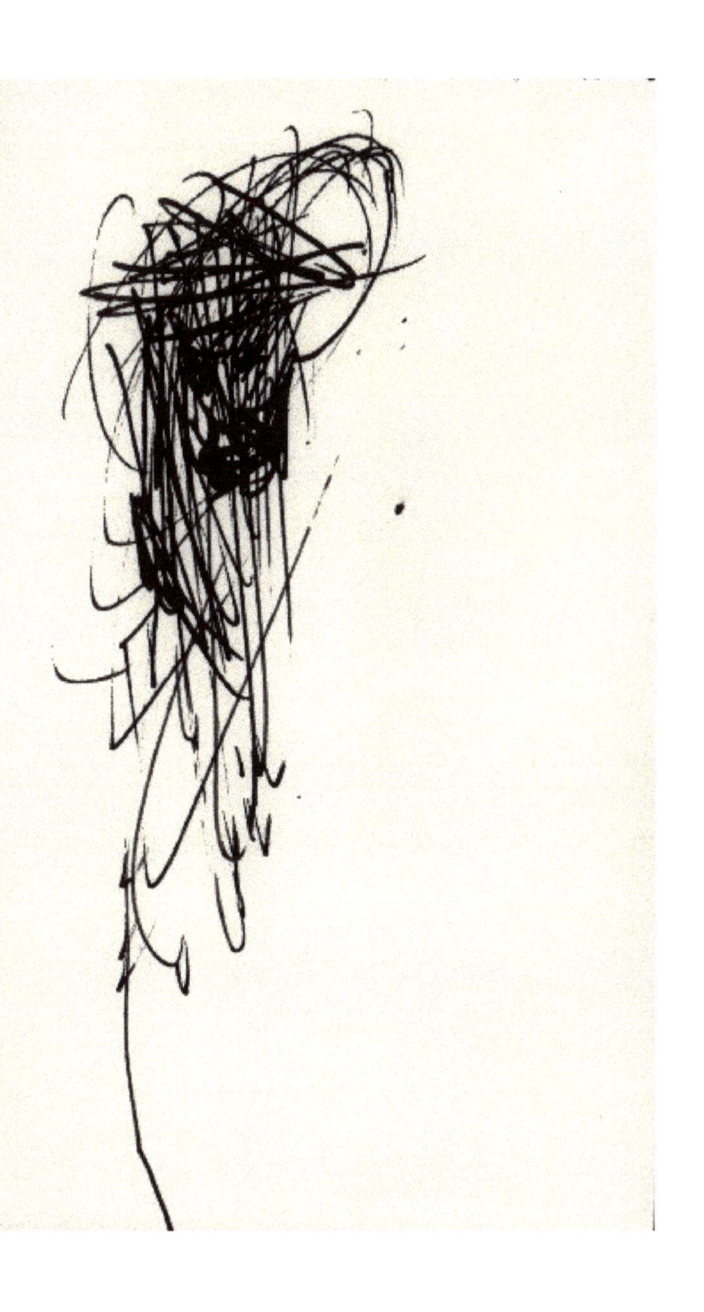

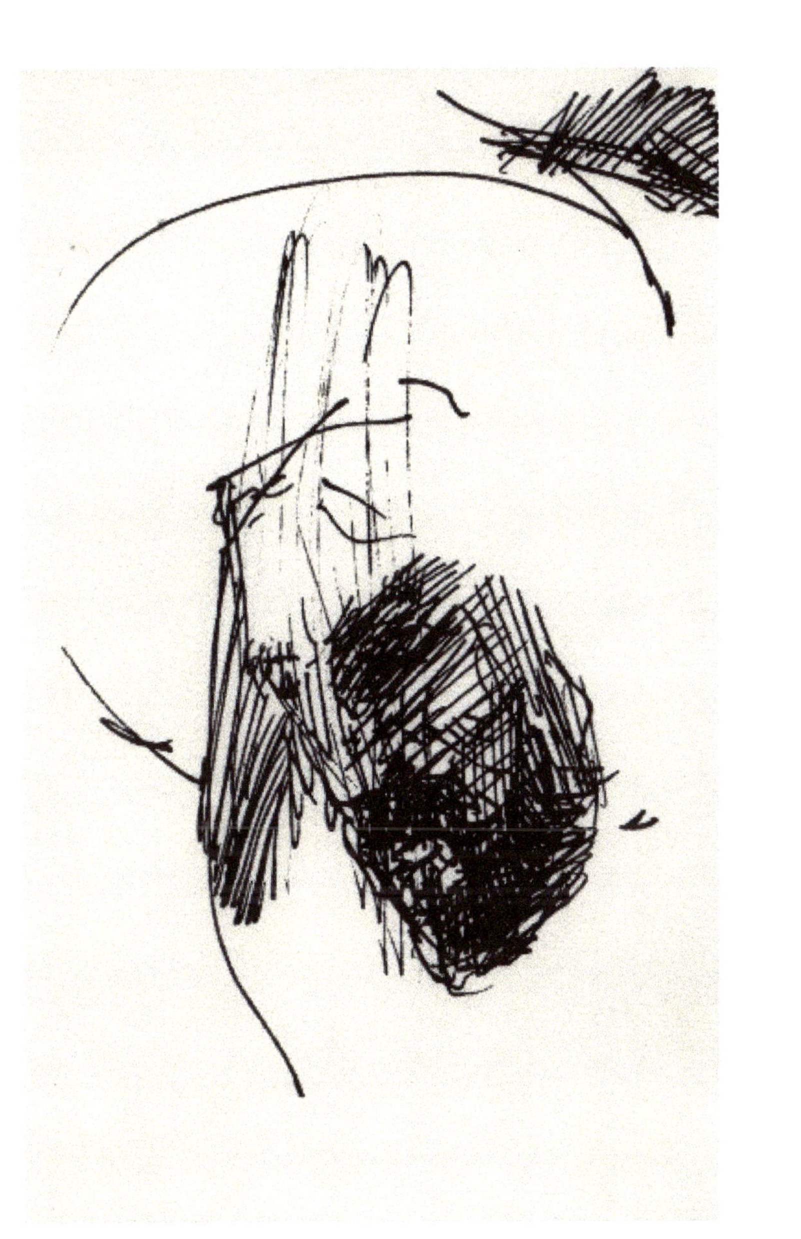

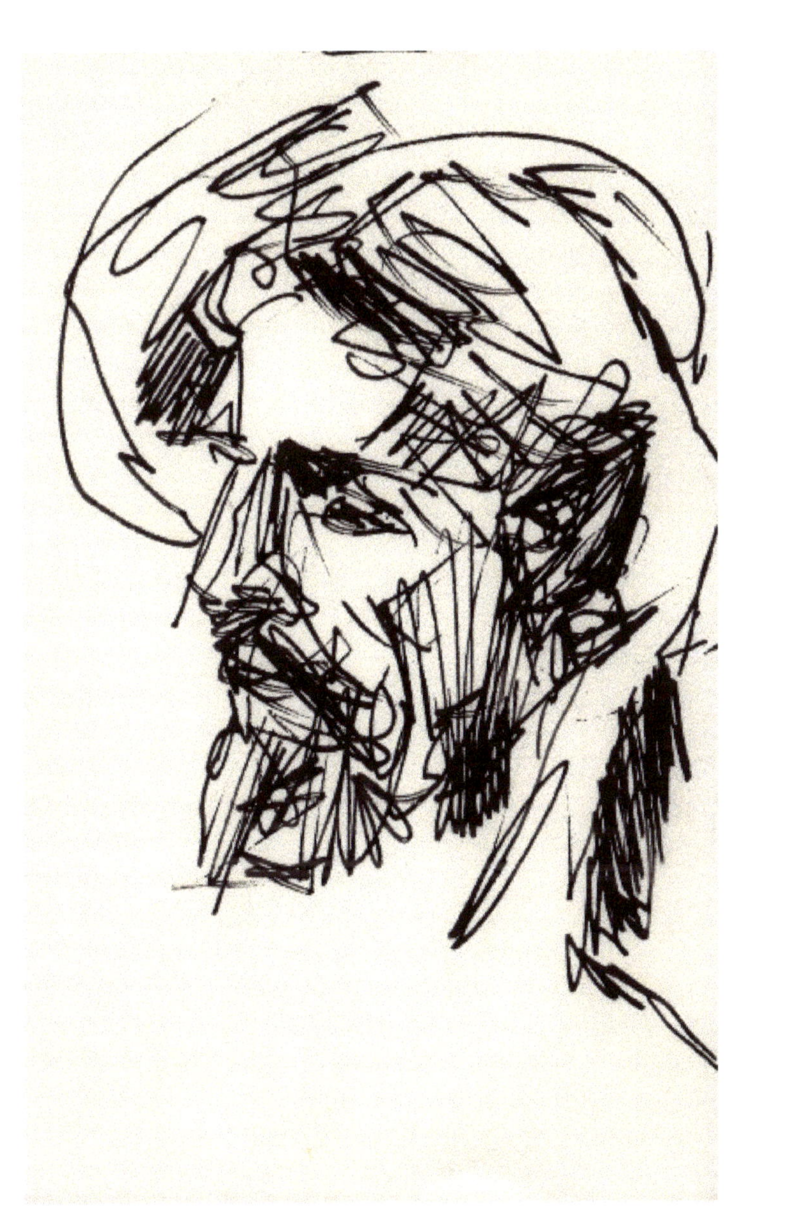

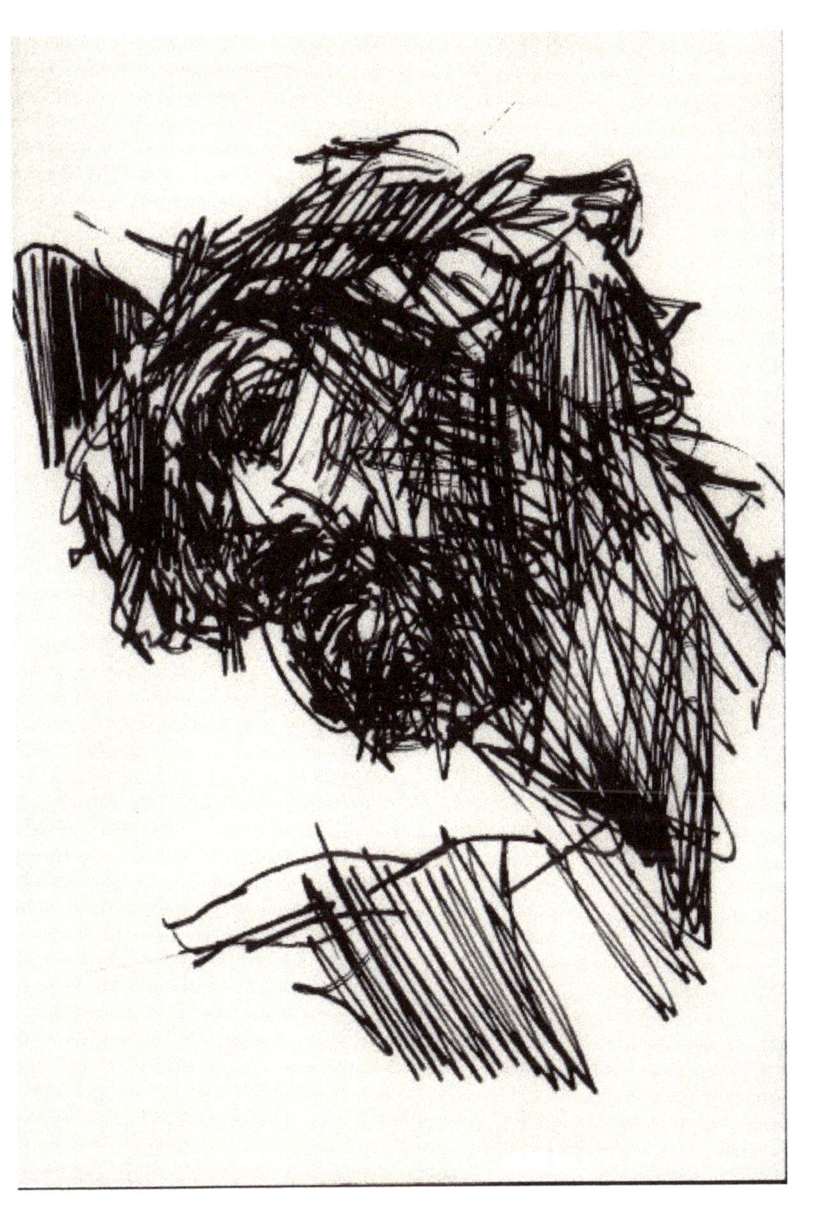

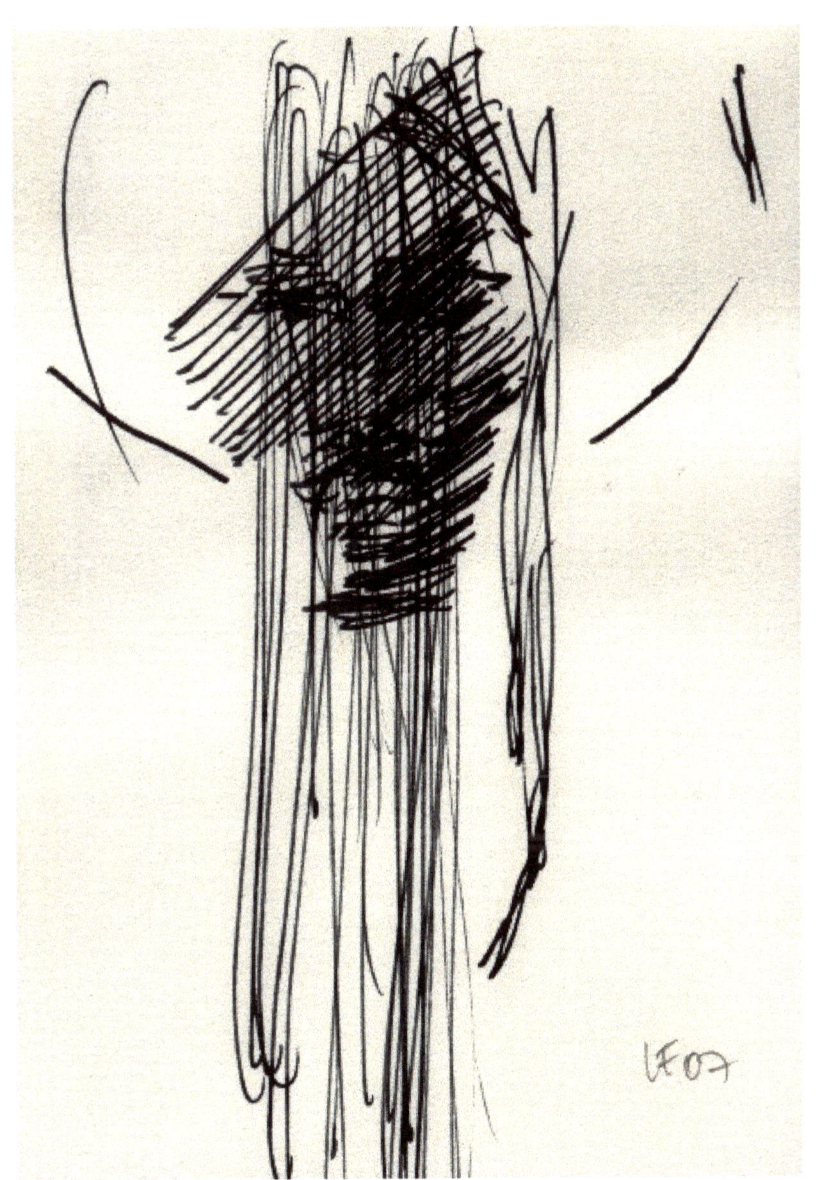

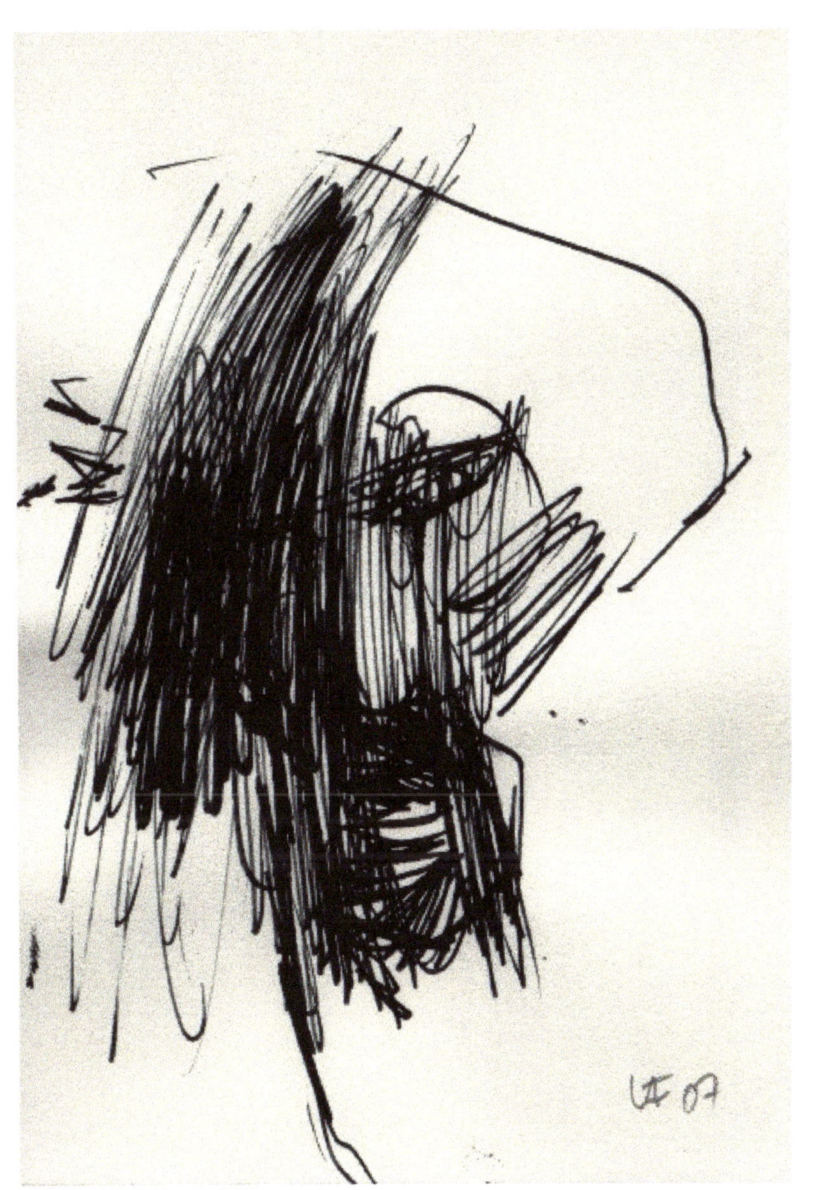

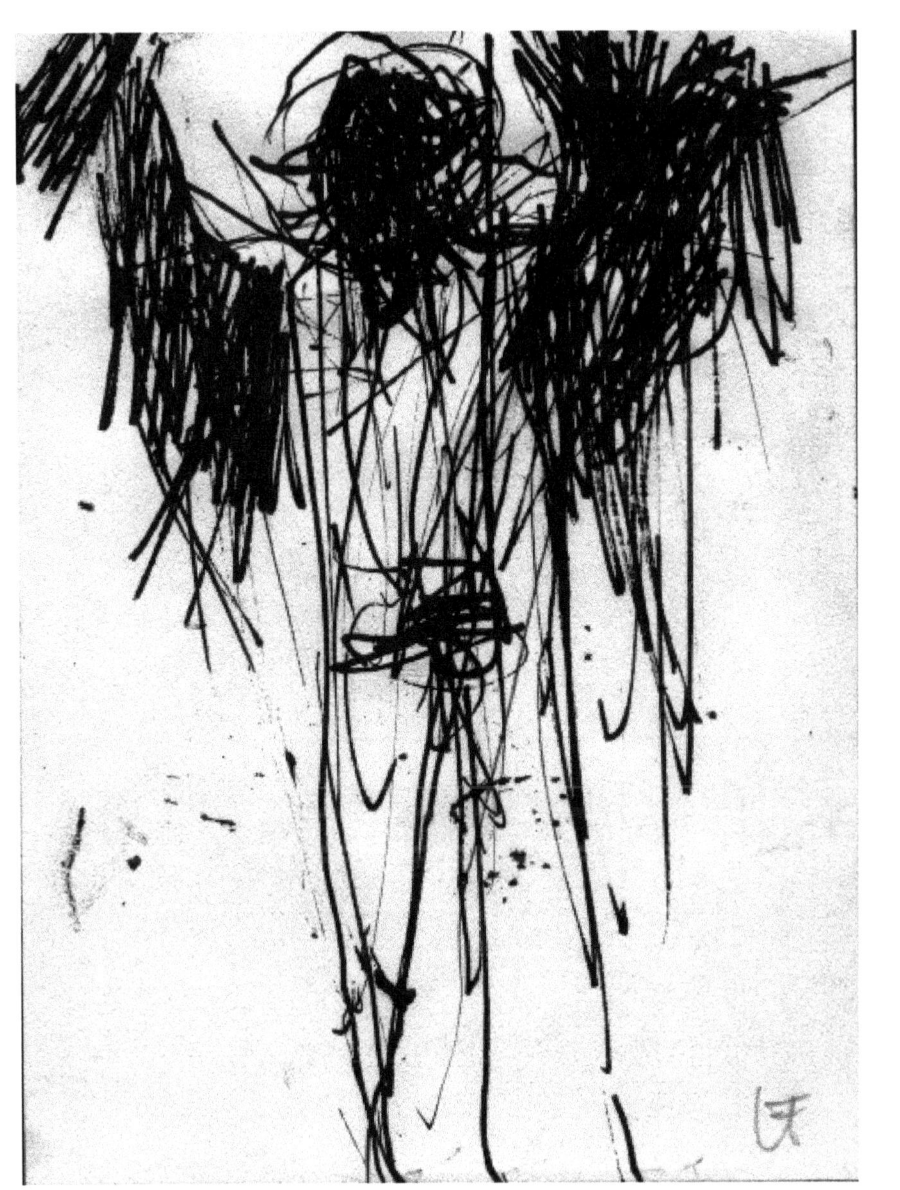

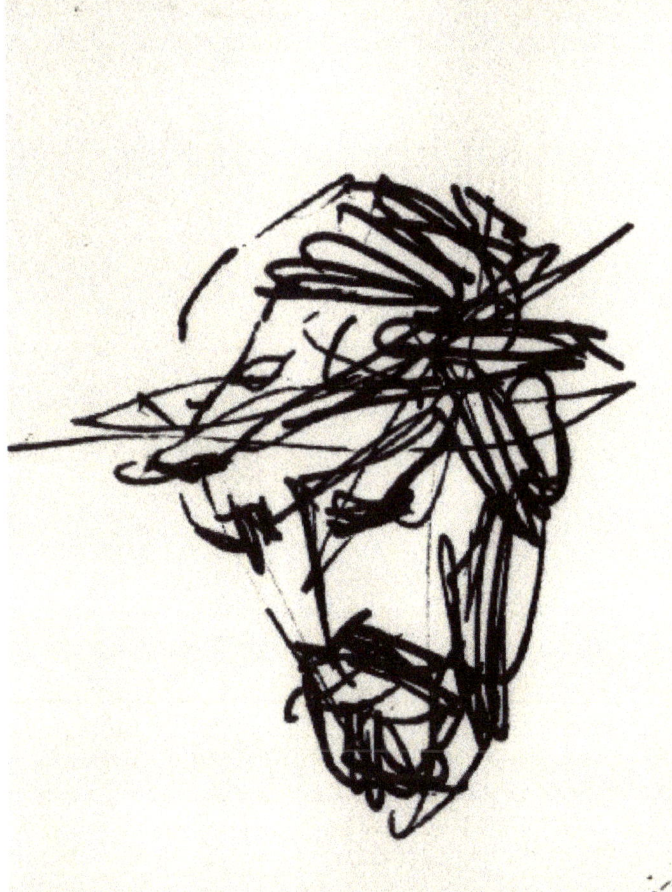

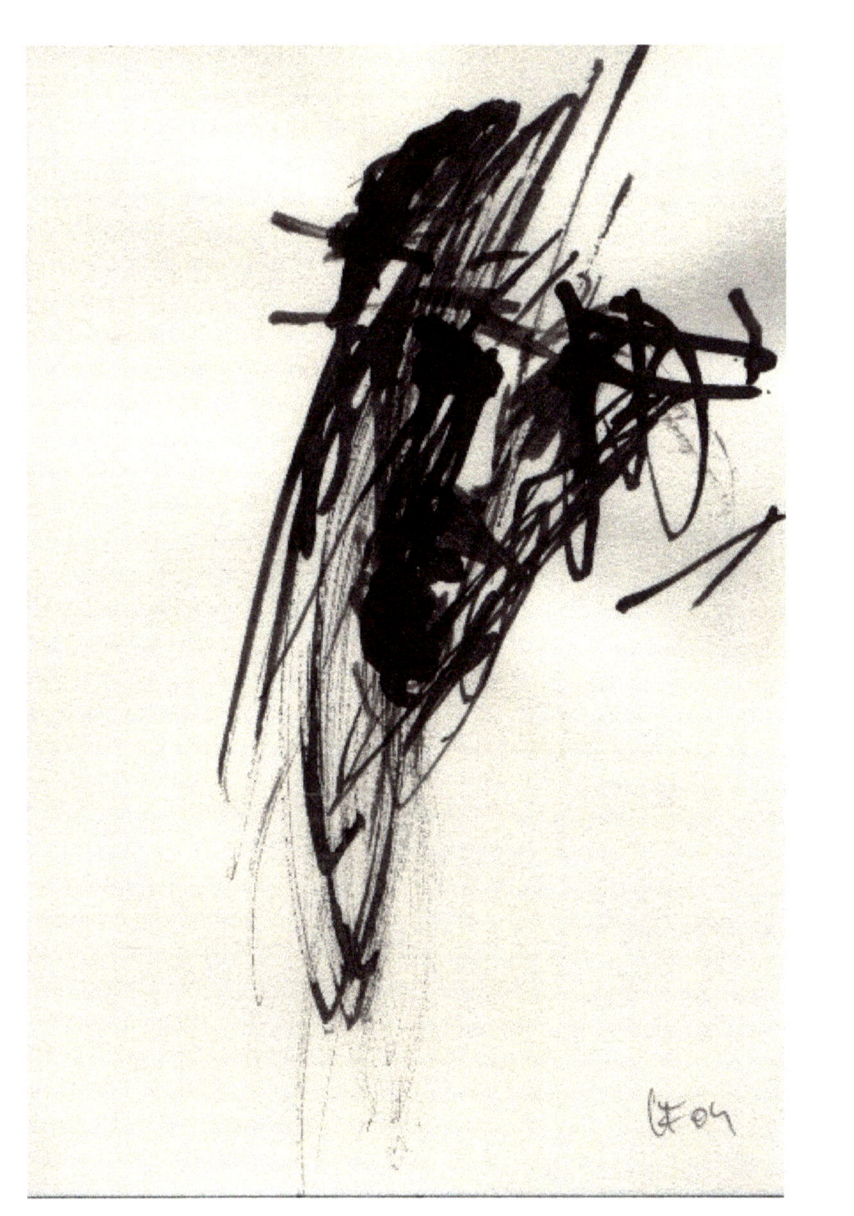

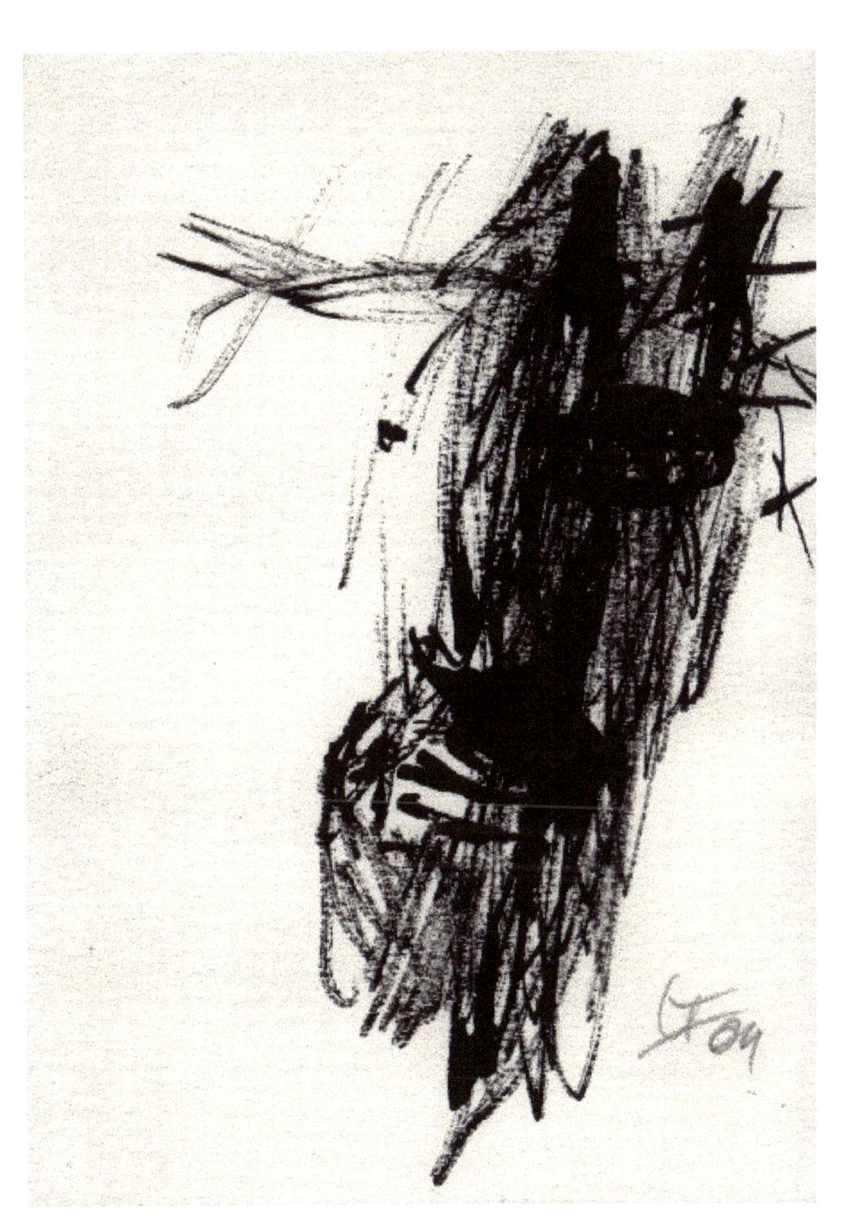

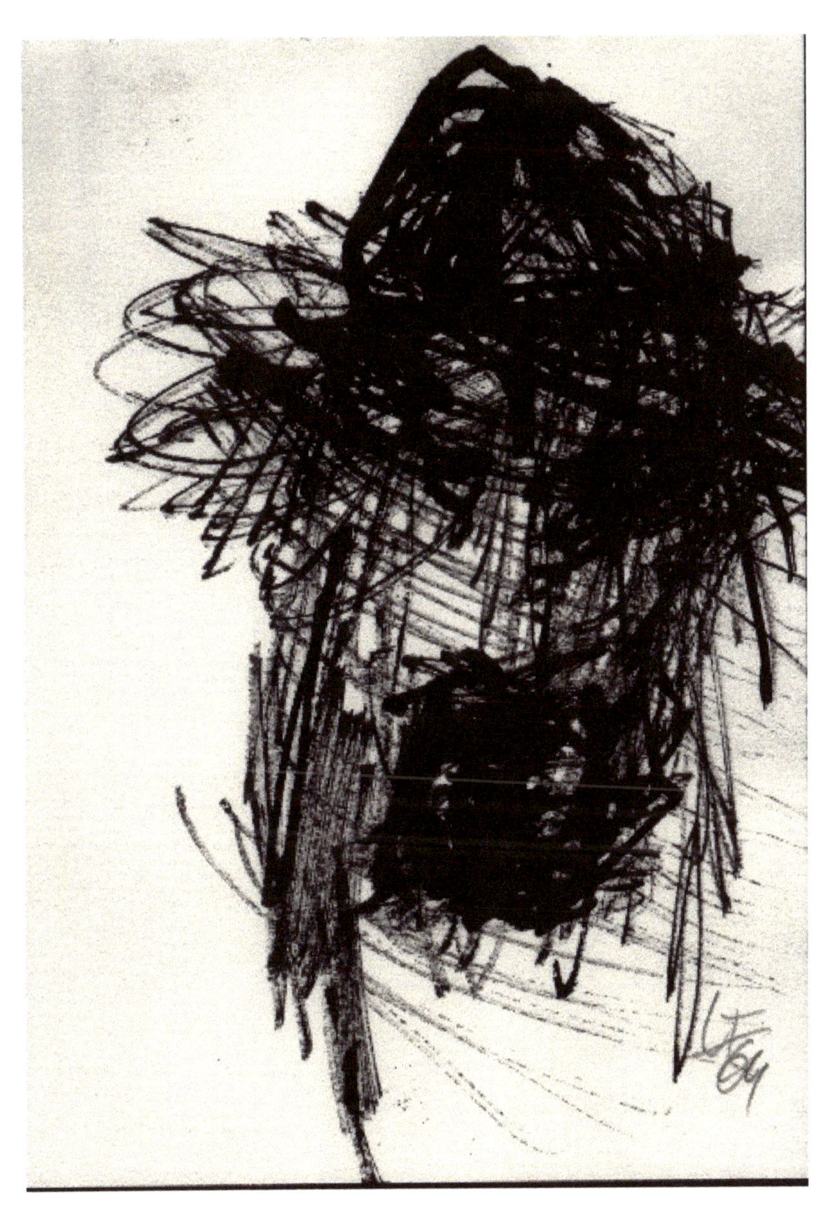

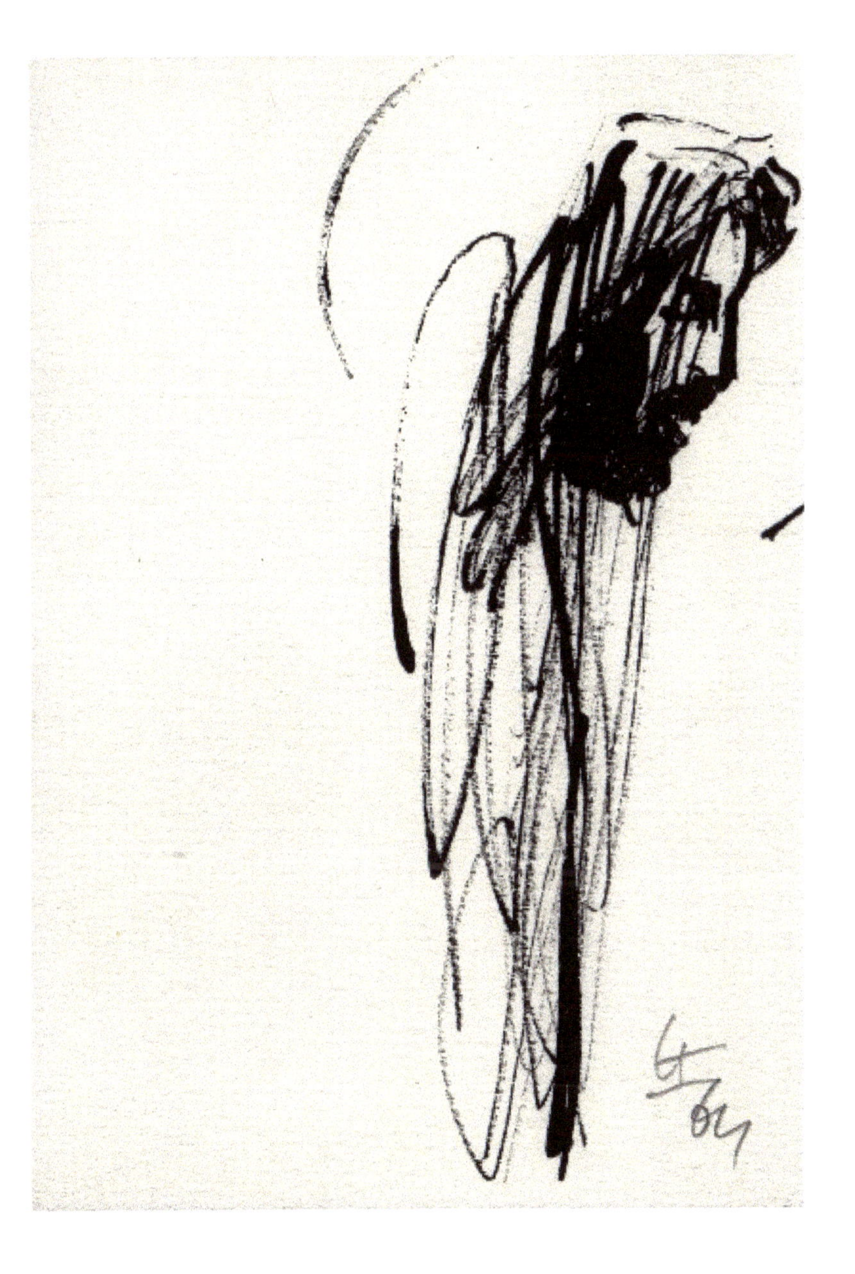

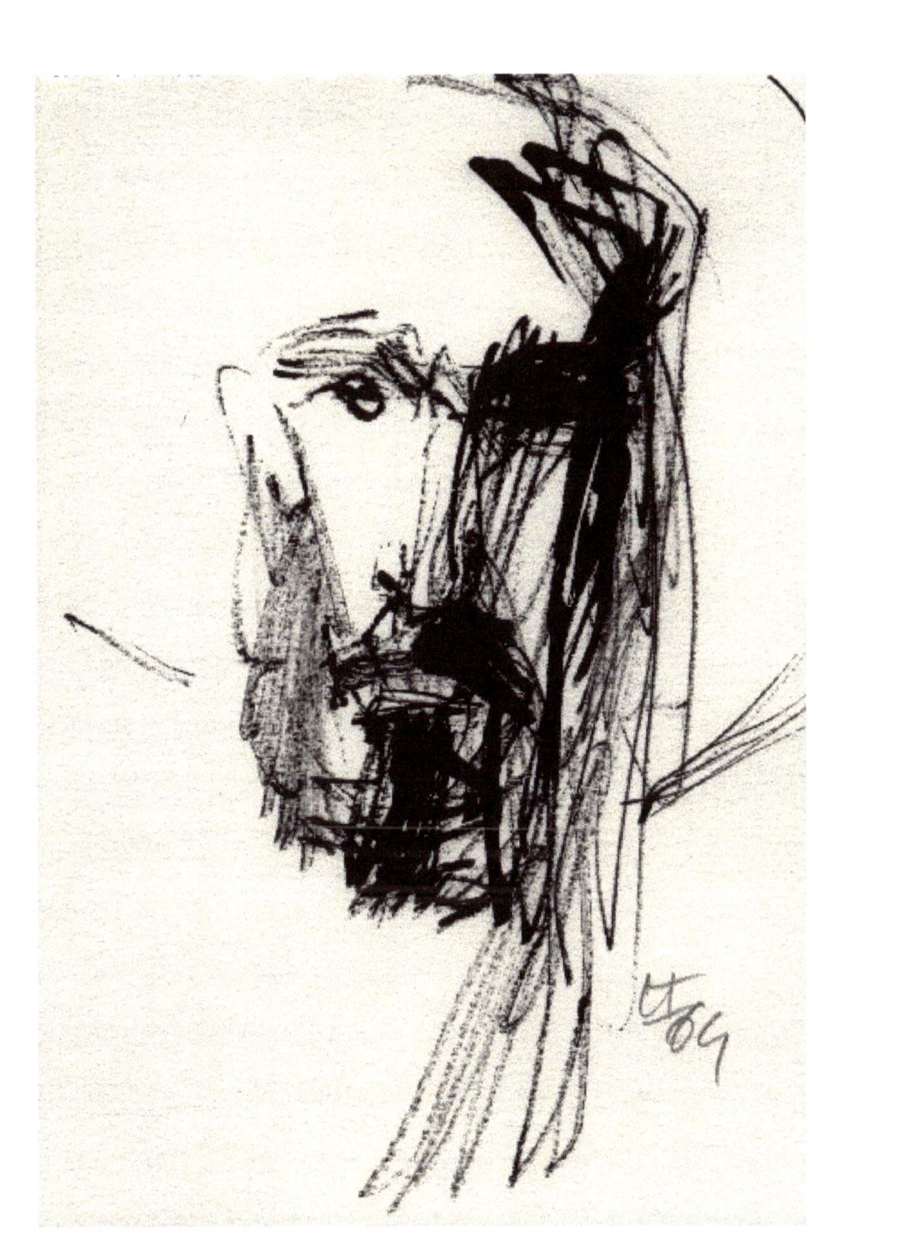

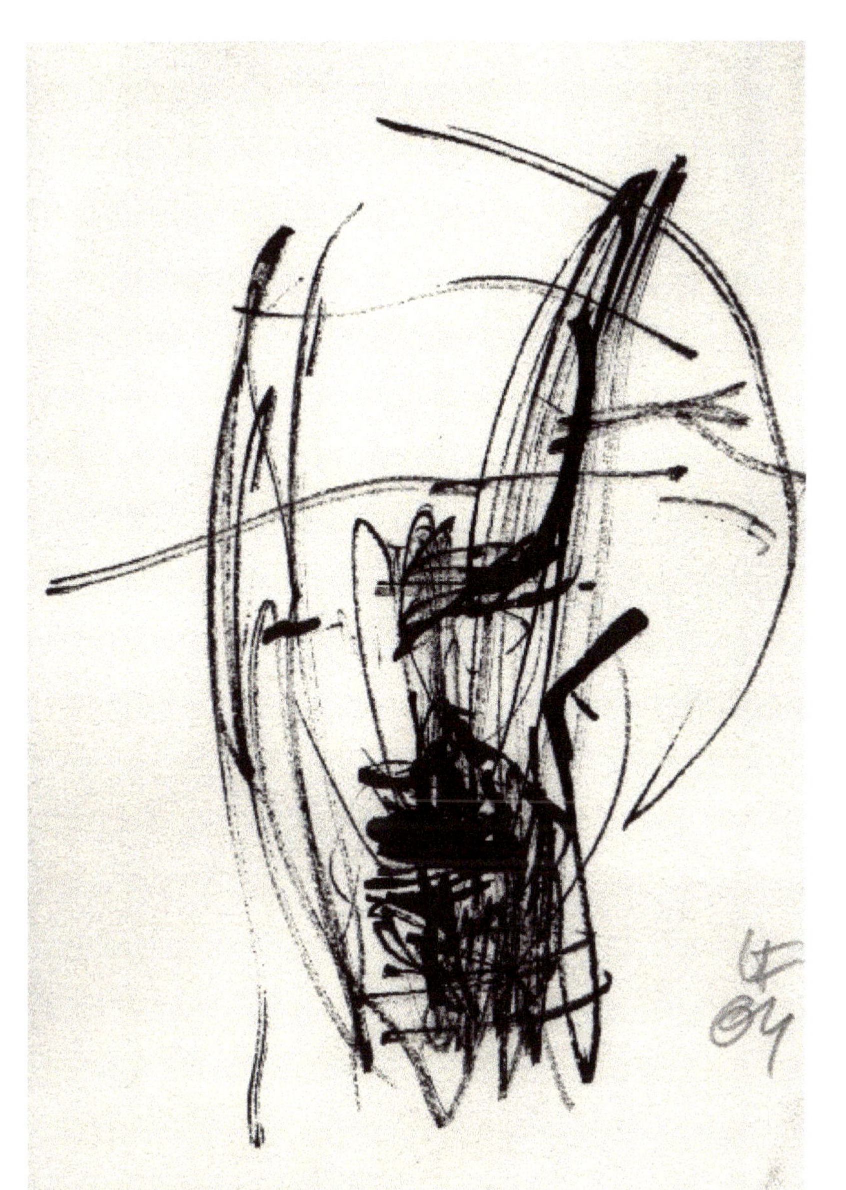

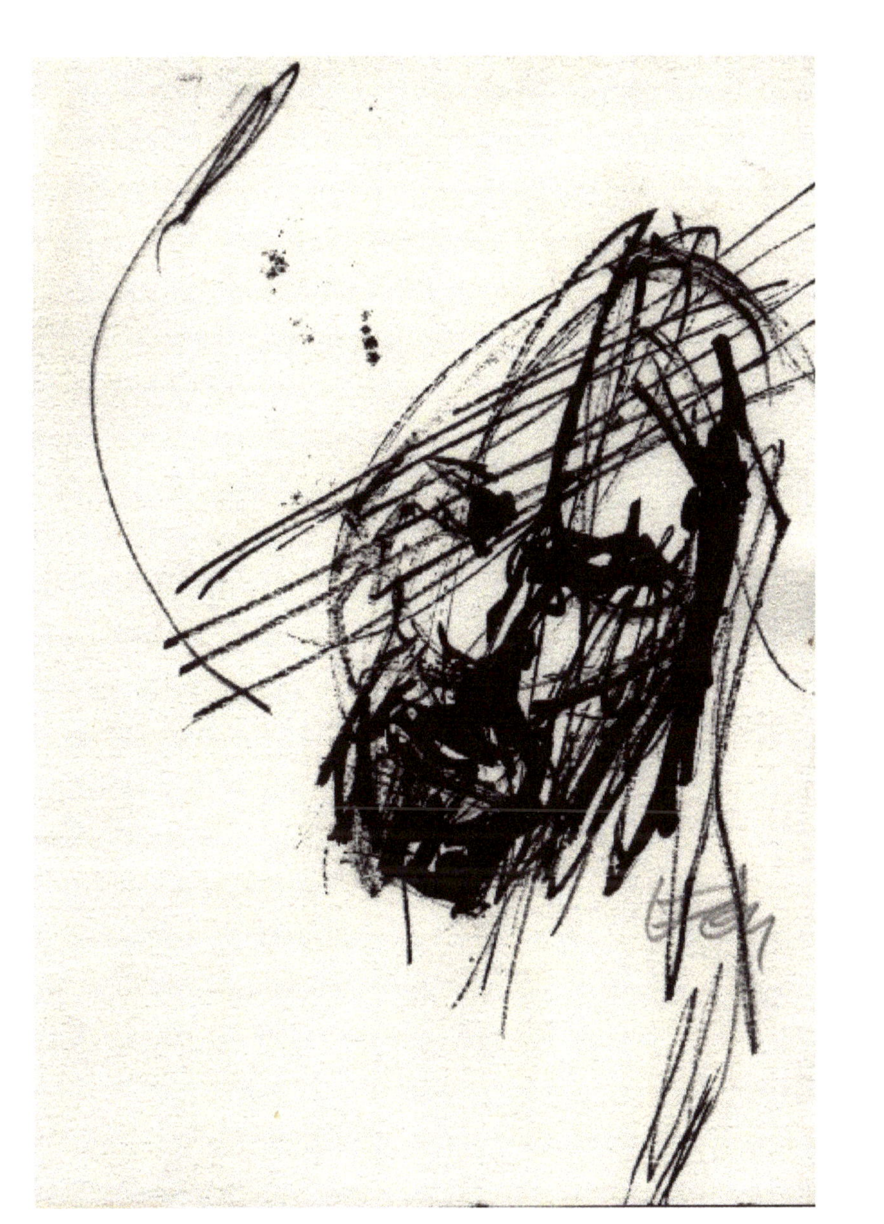

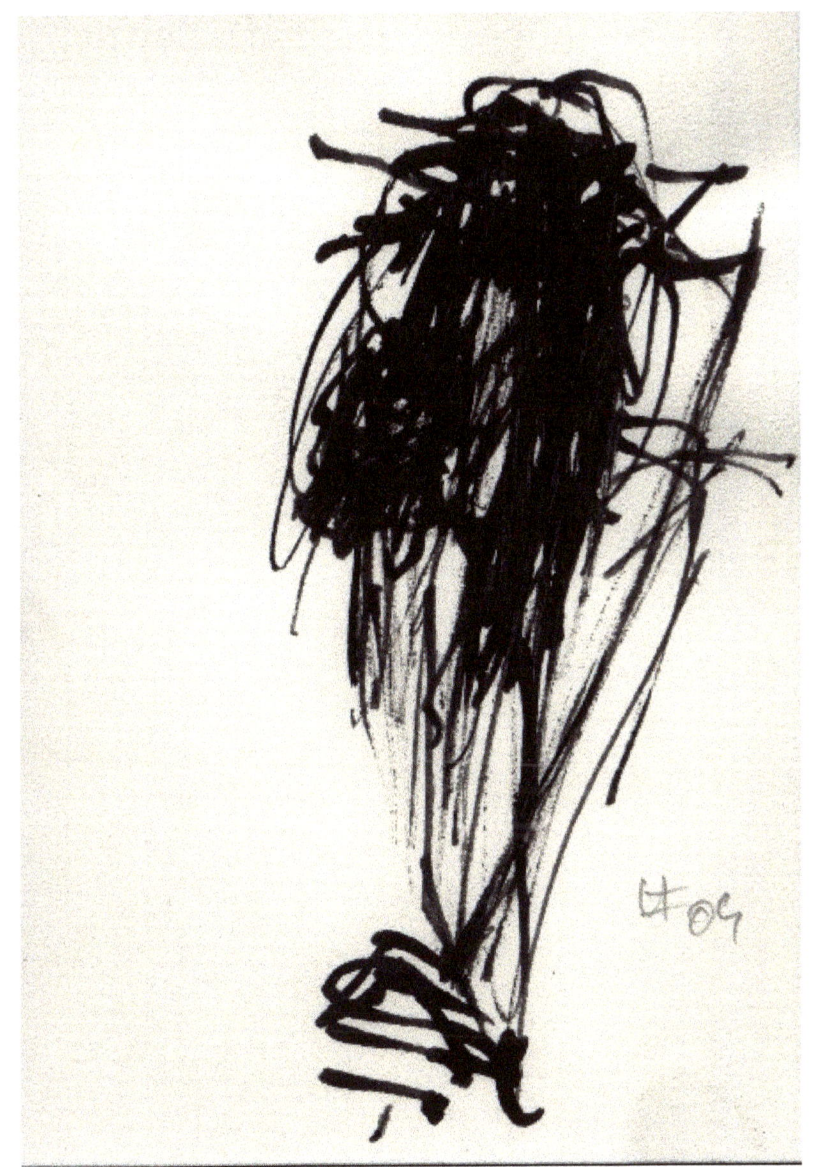

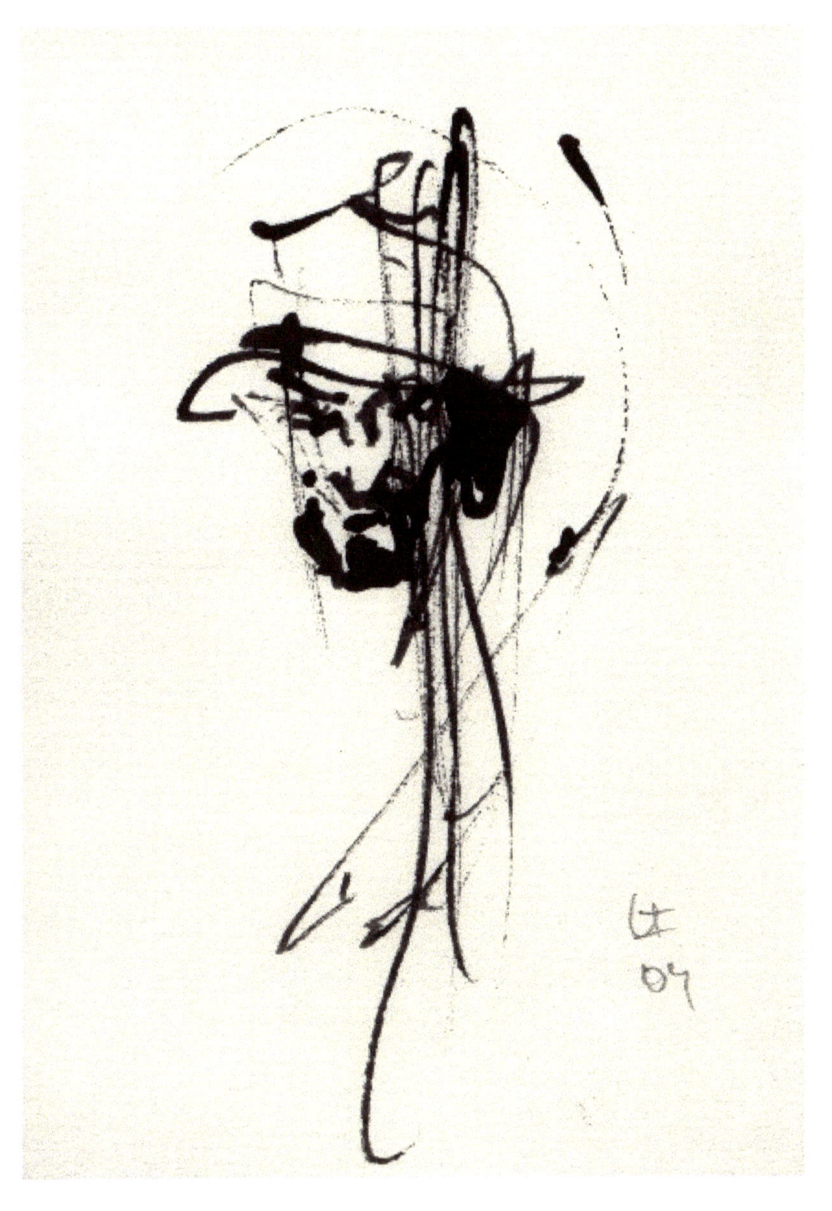

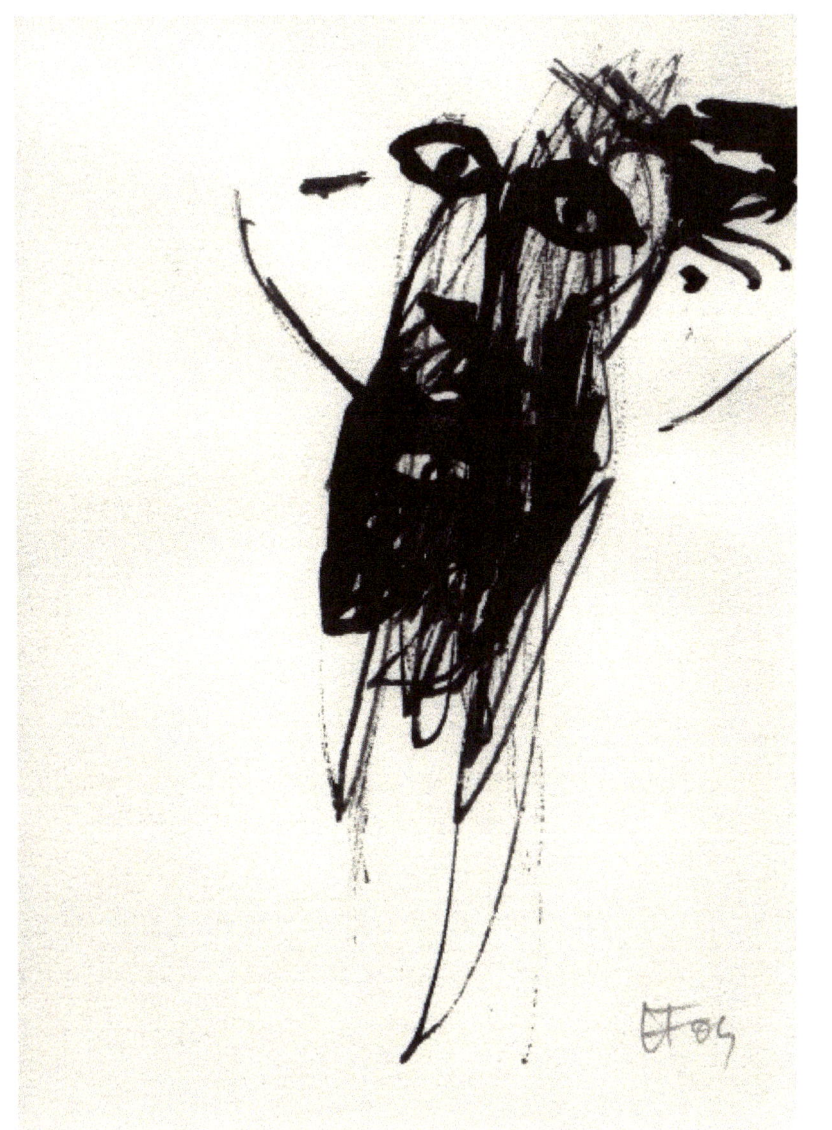

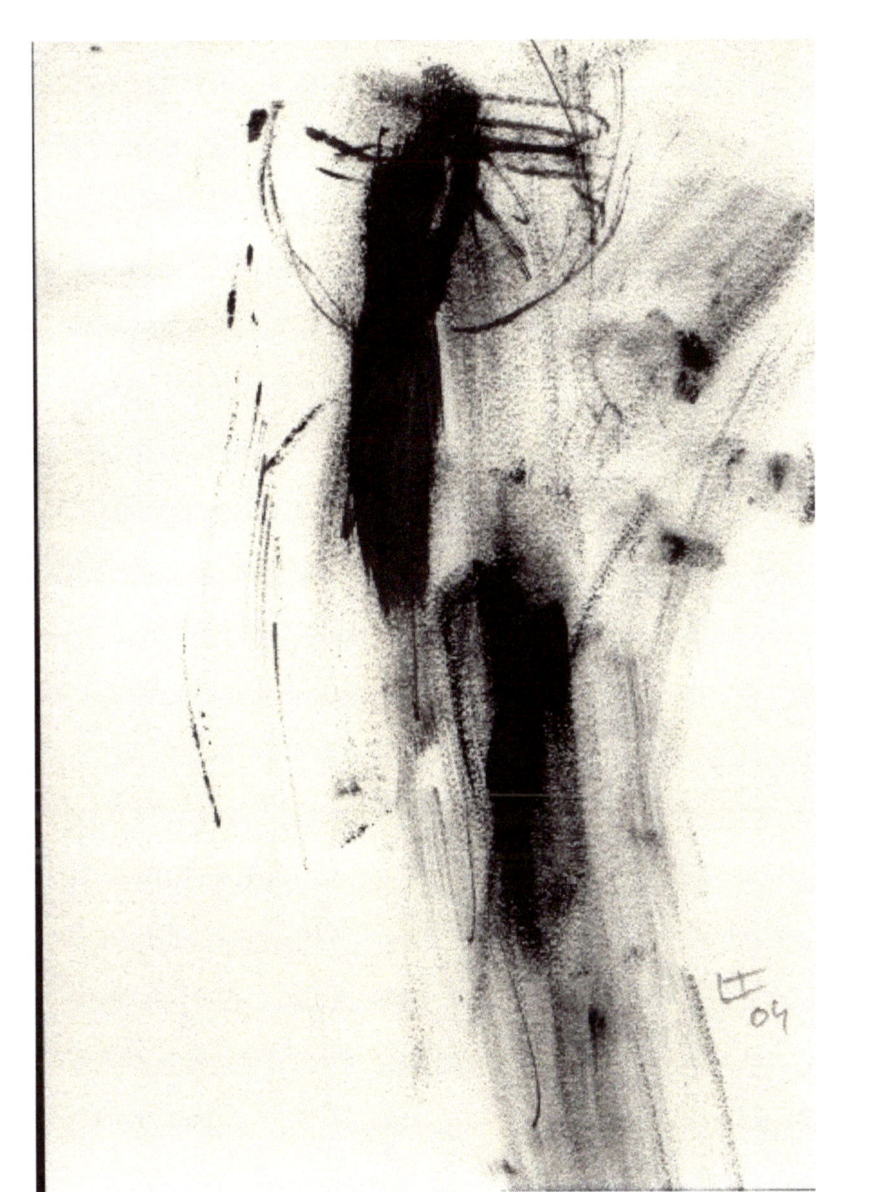

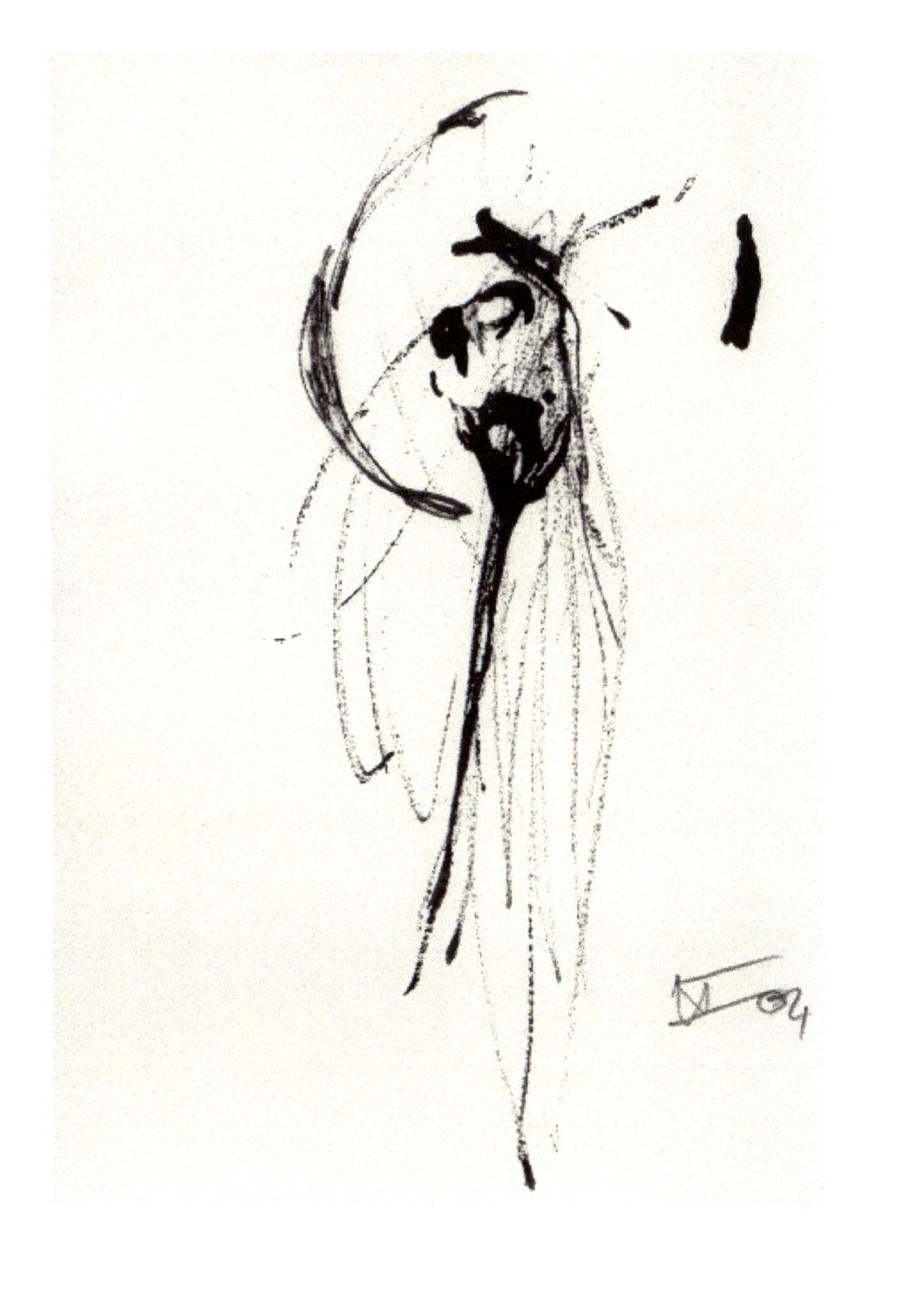

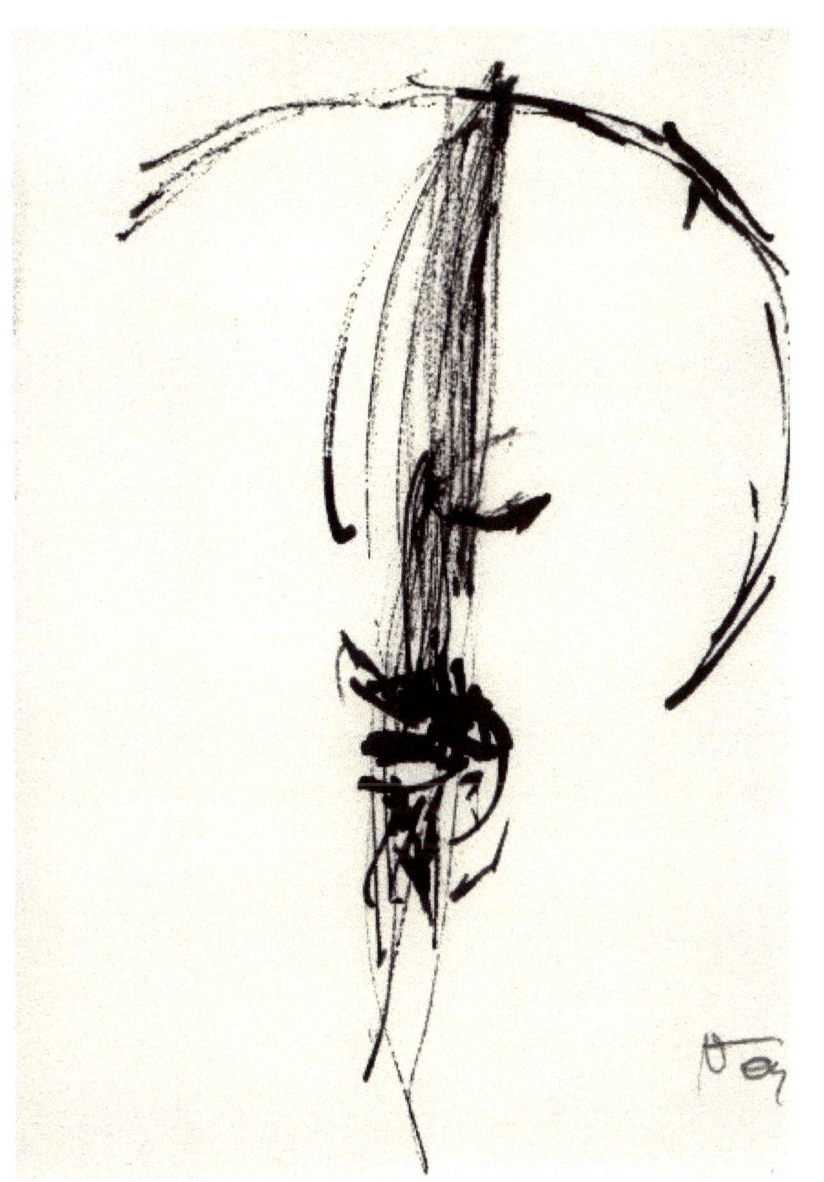

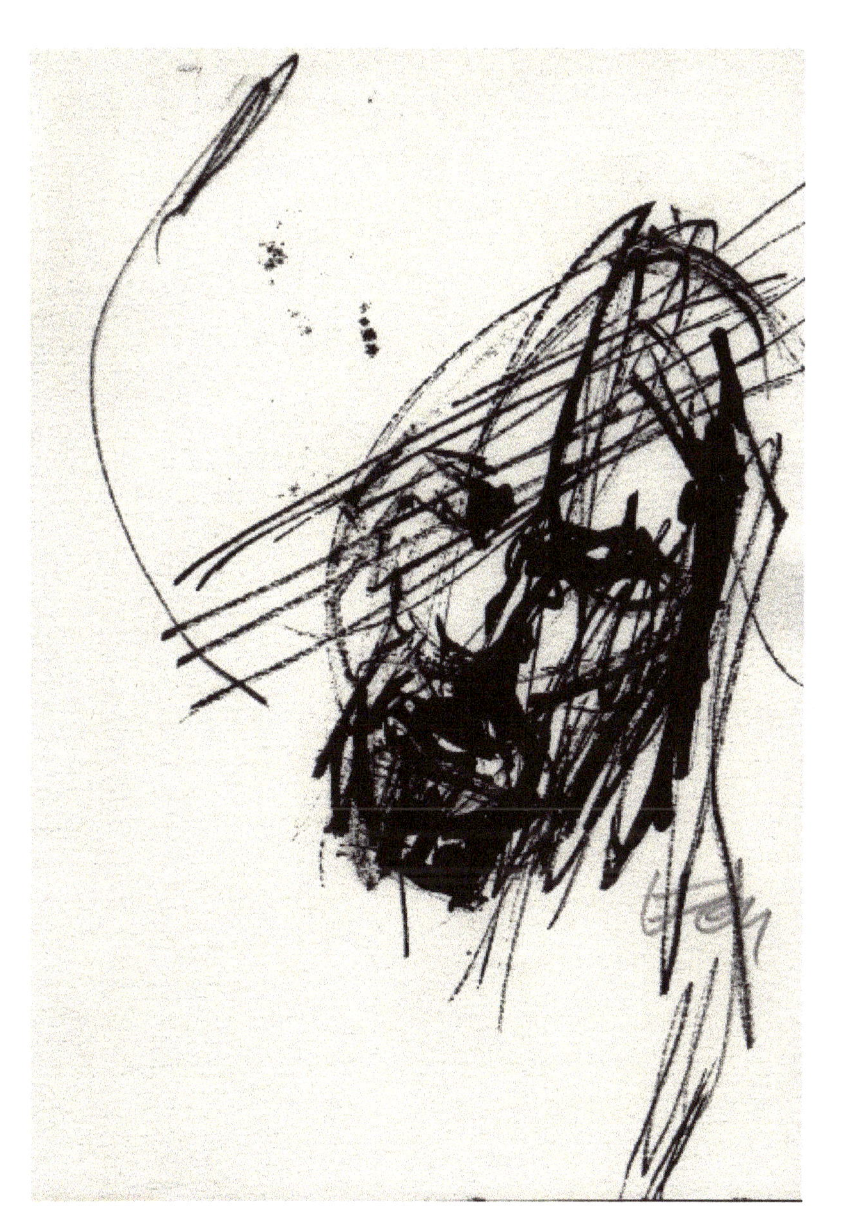

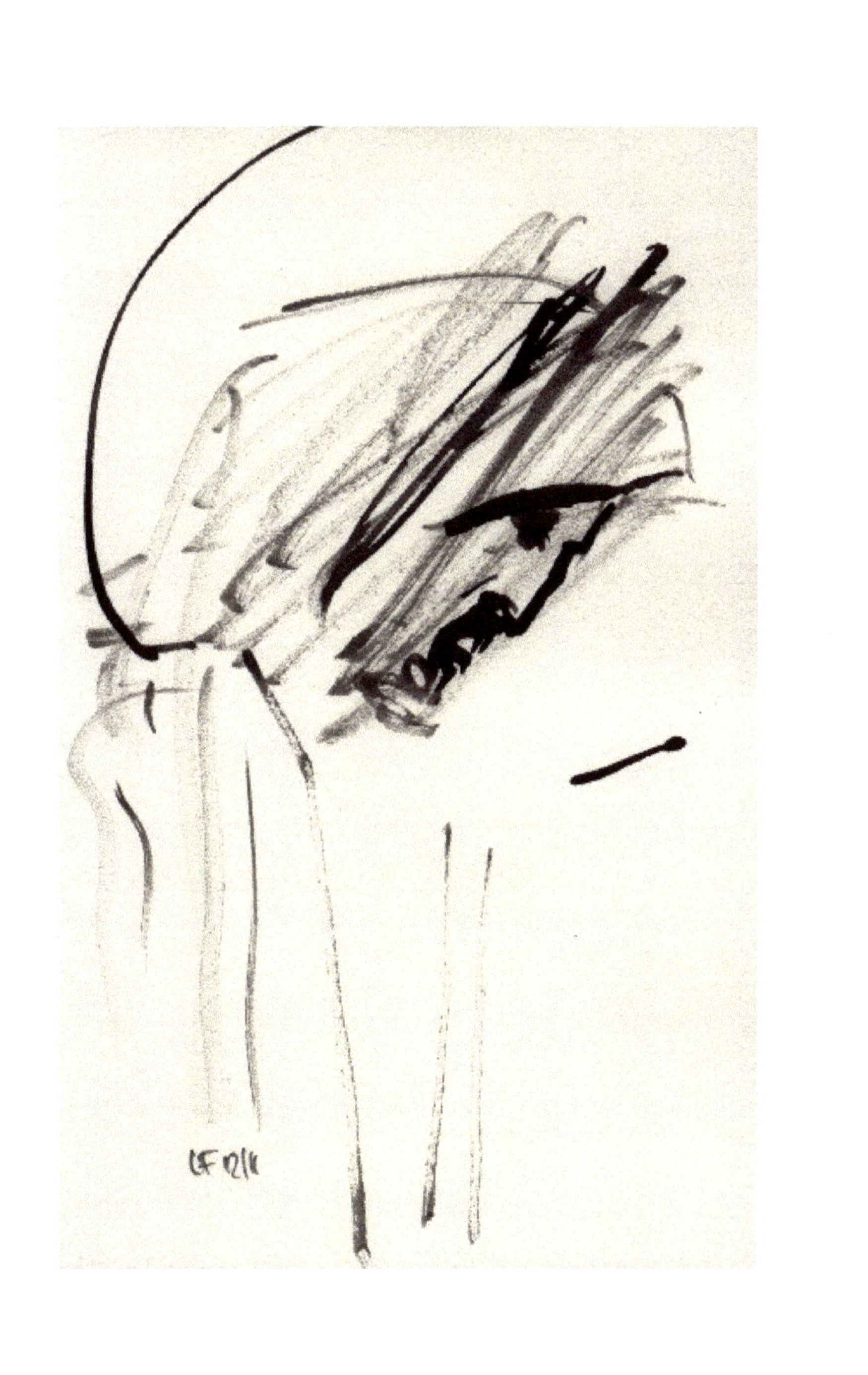

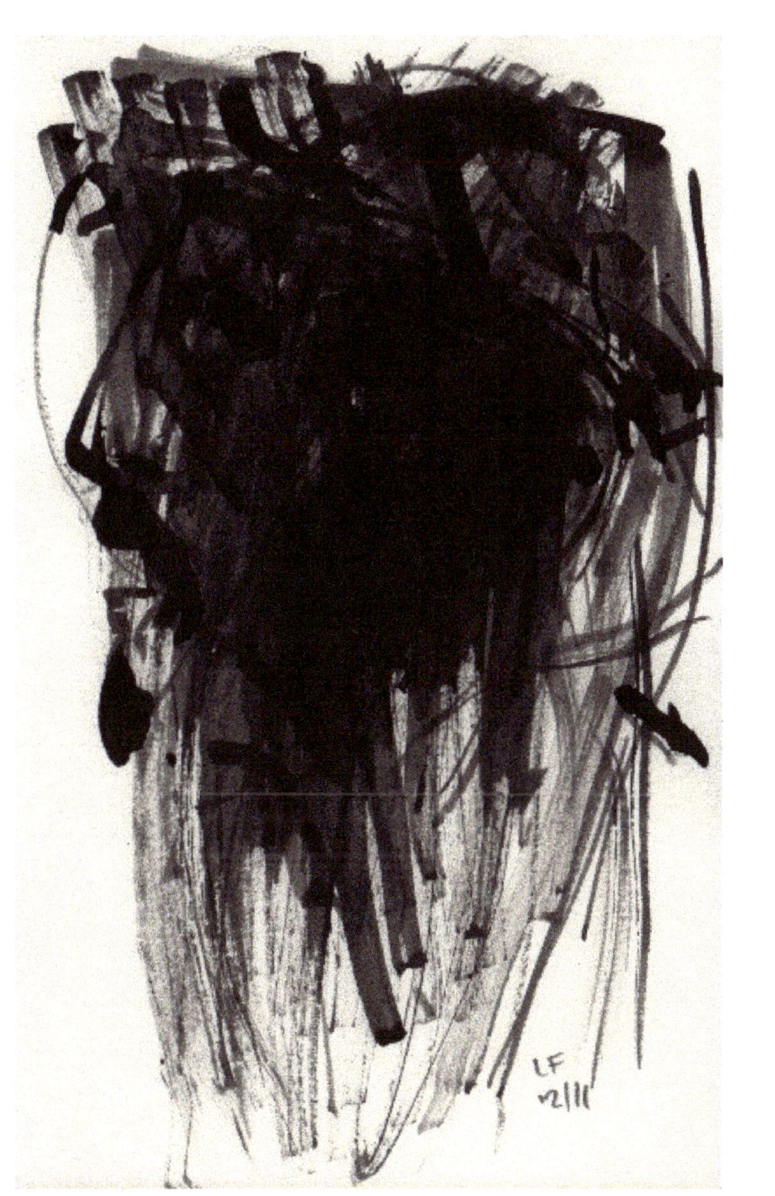
LF
2/11

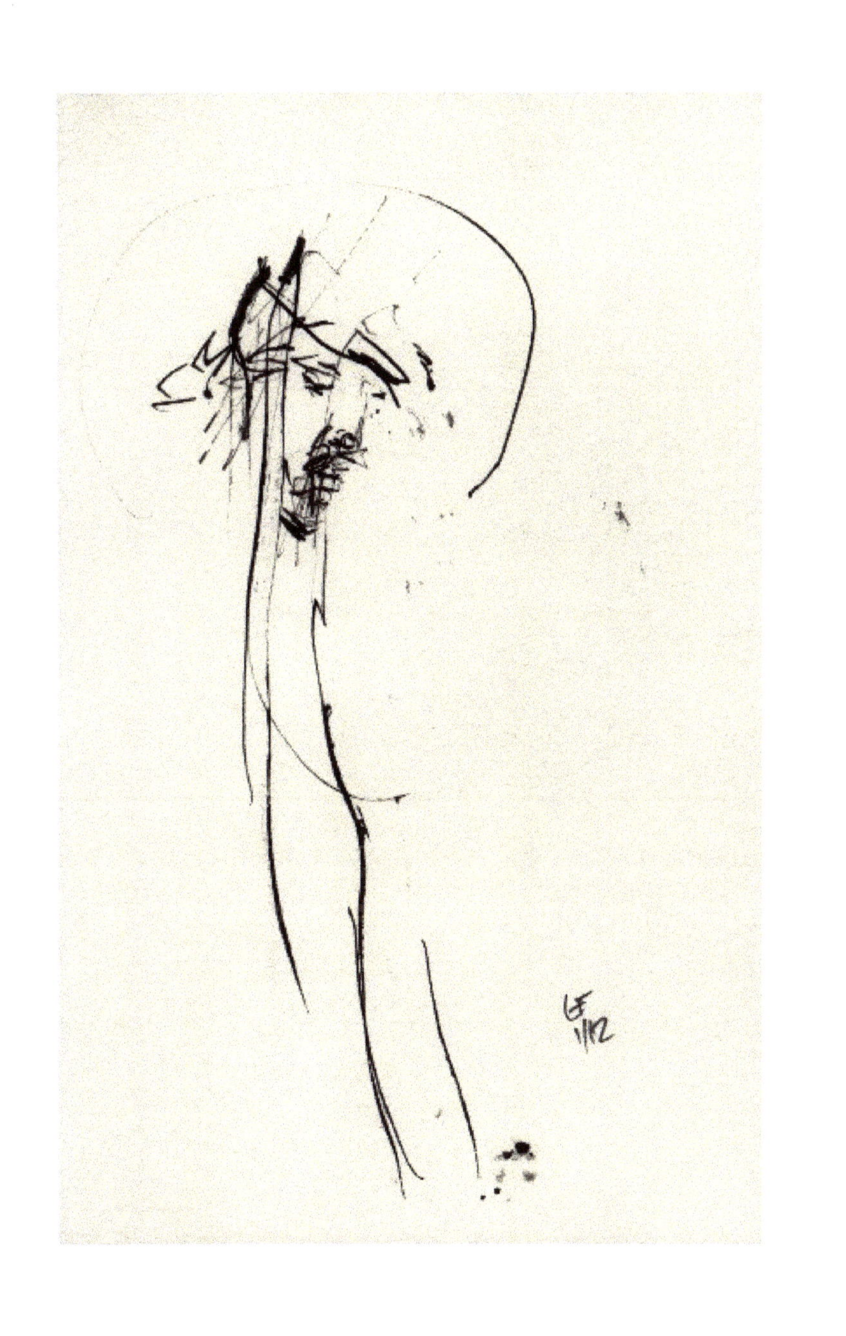

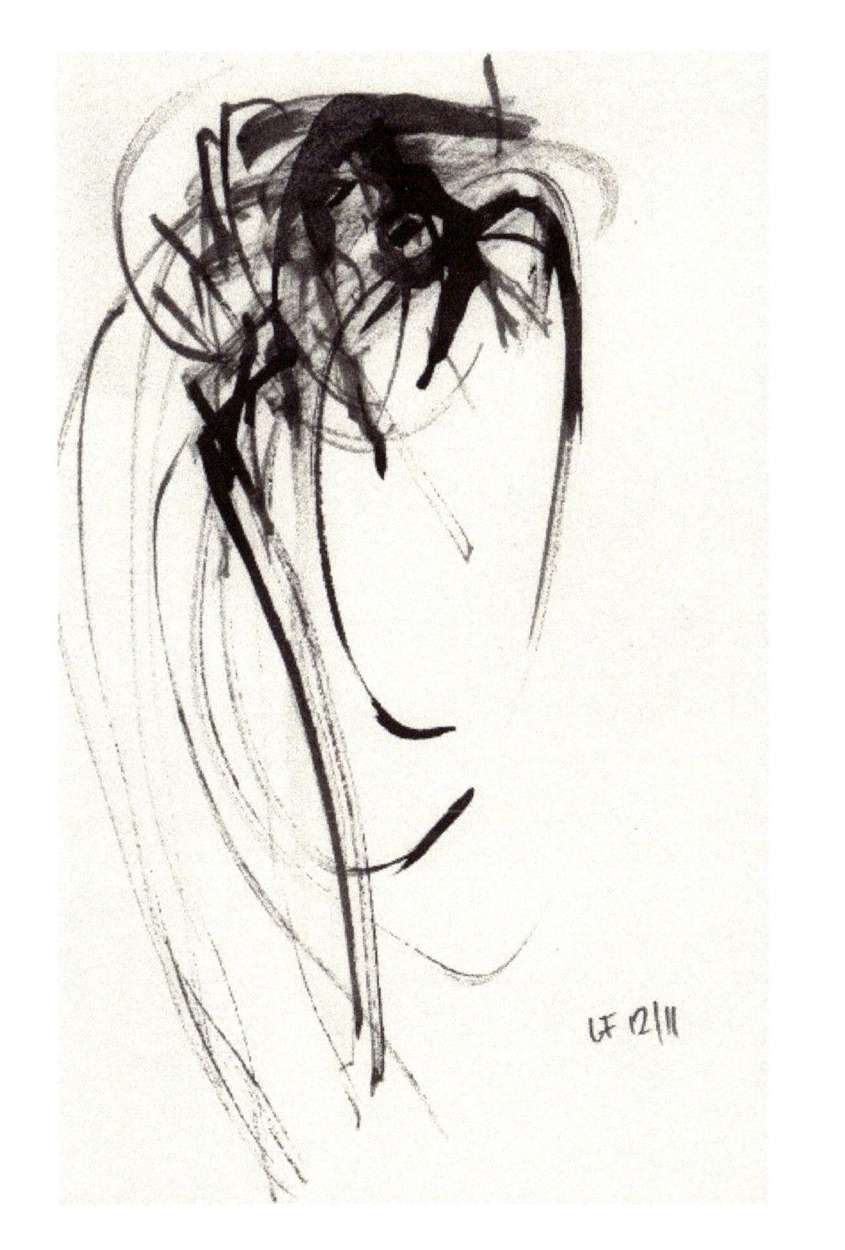
LF 12|11

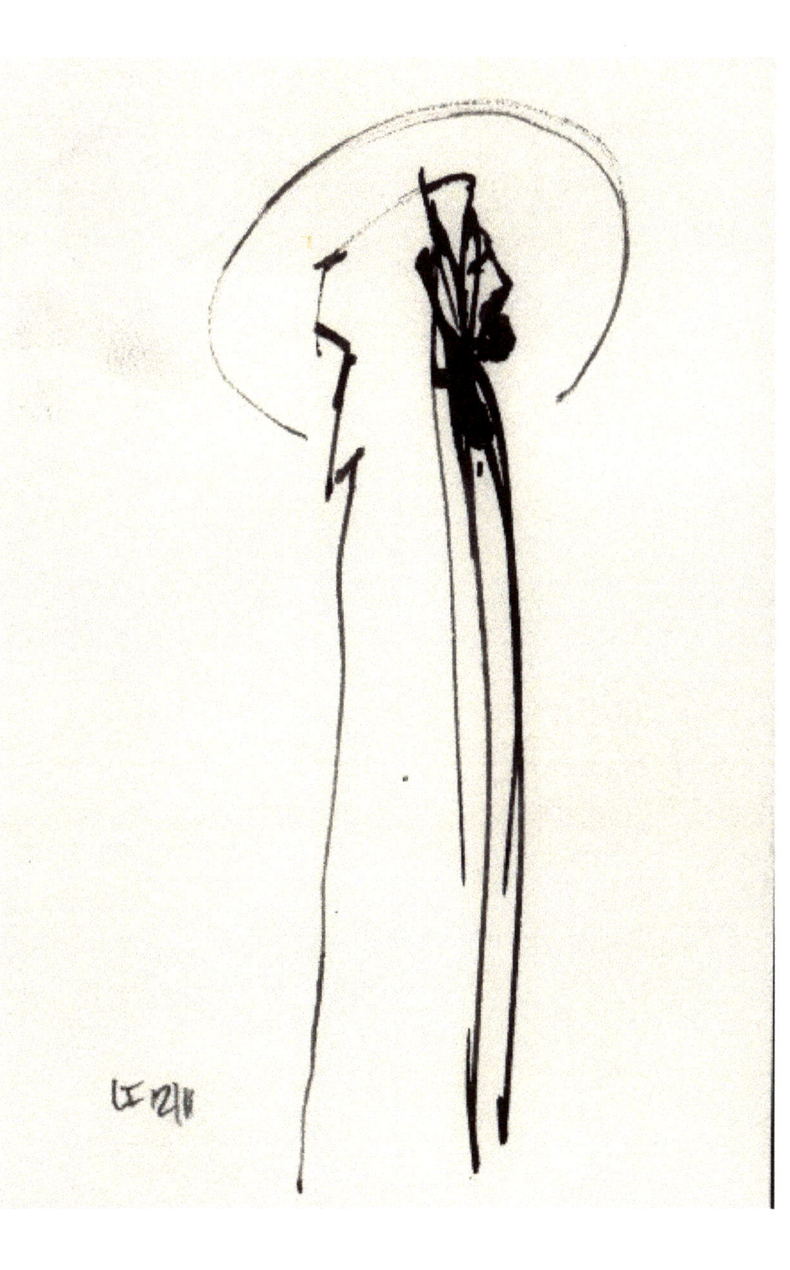

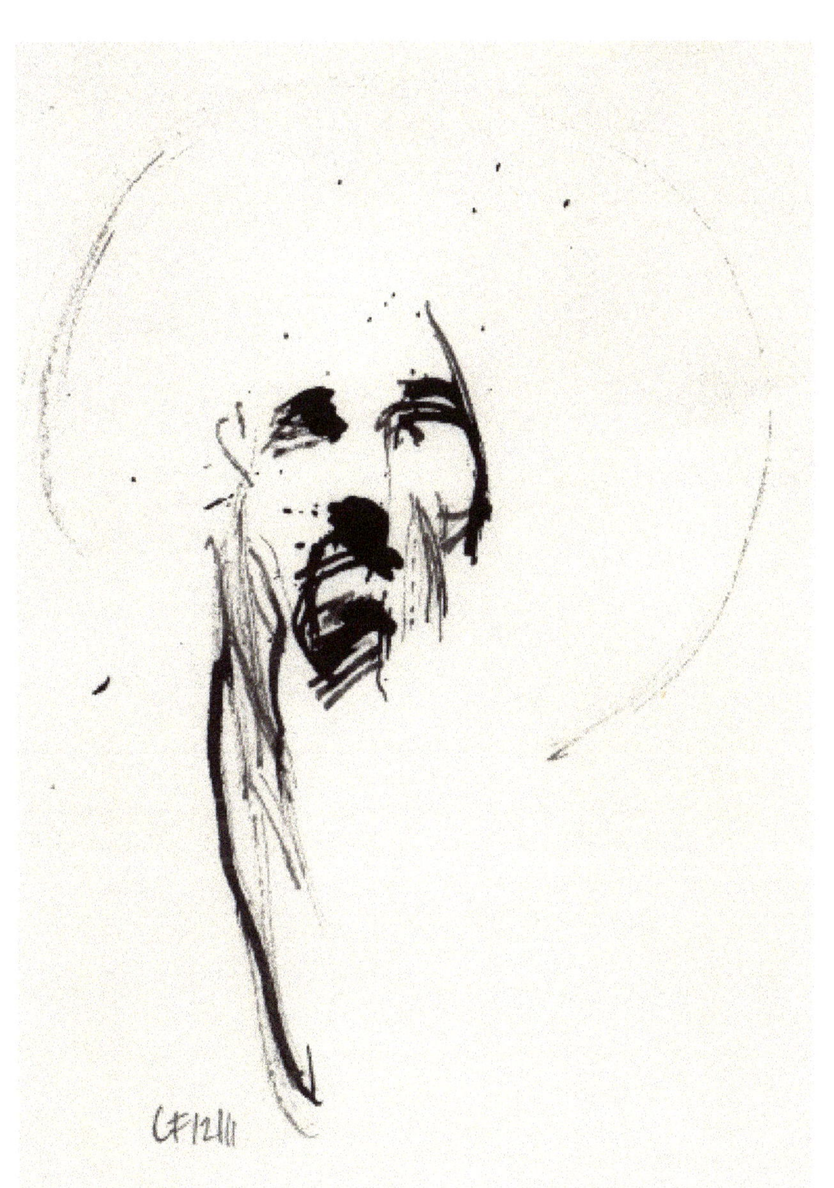

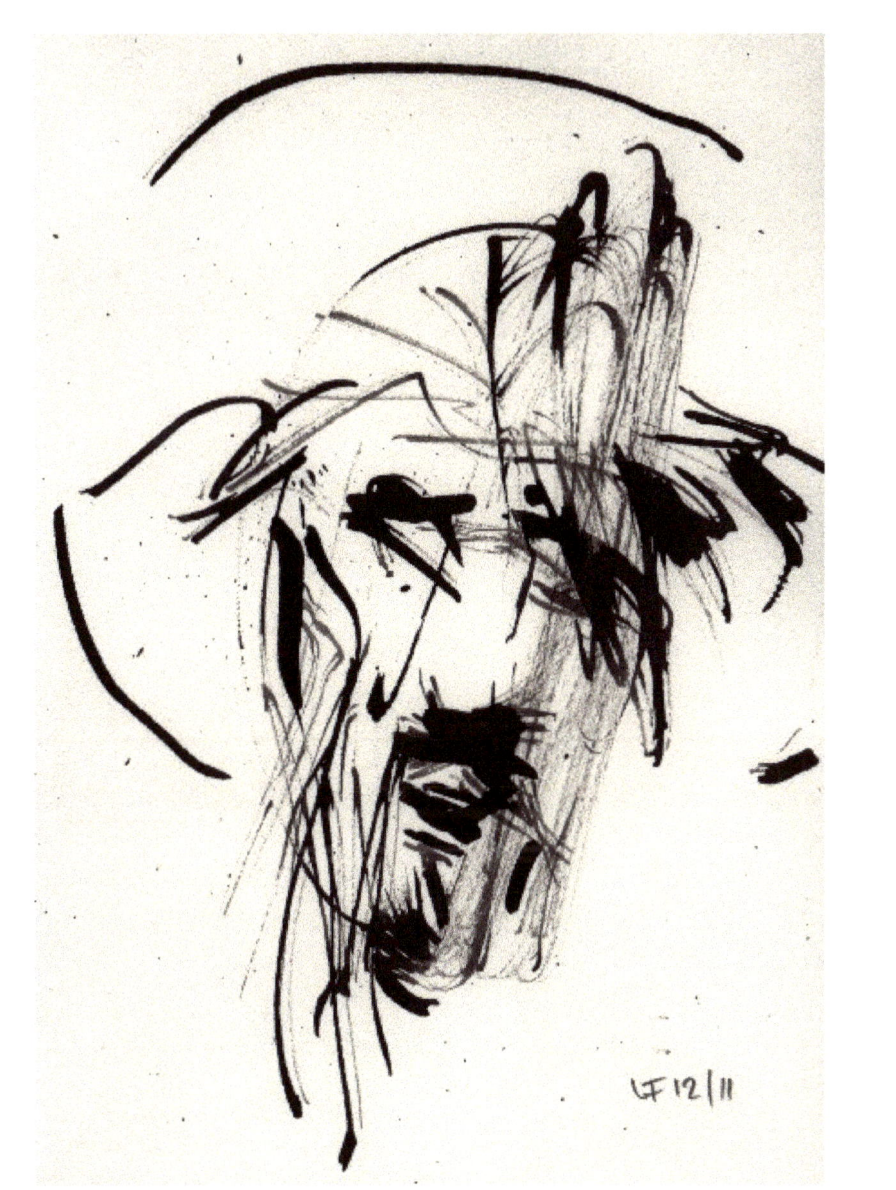
LF 12/11

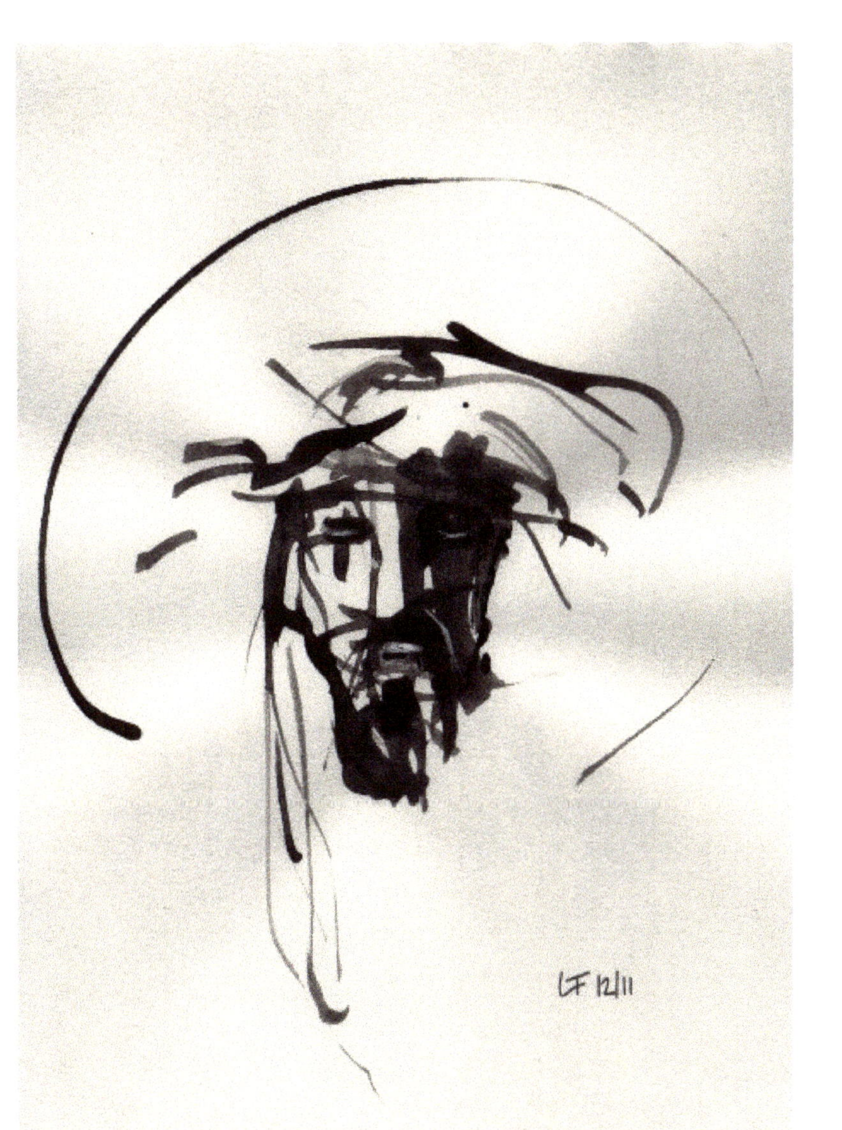

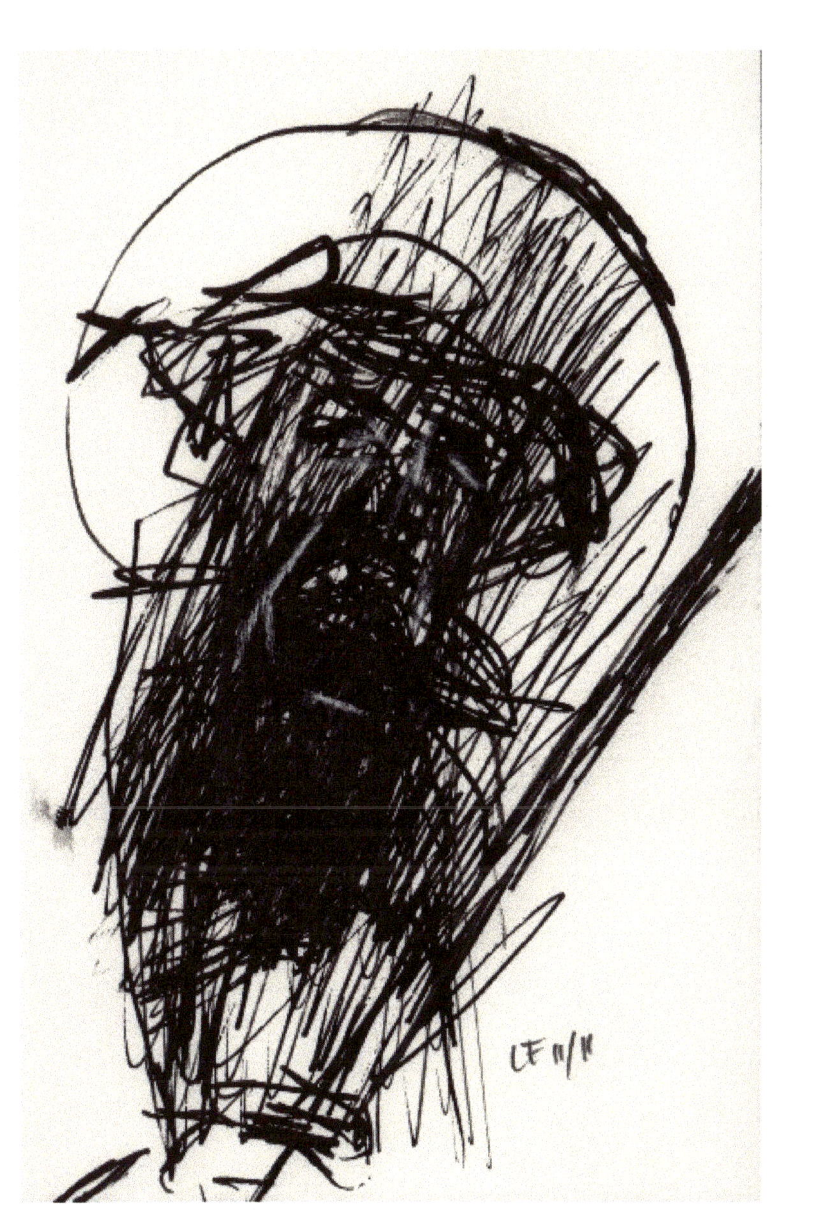
LF 11/11

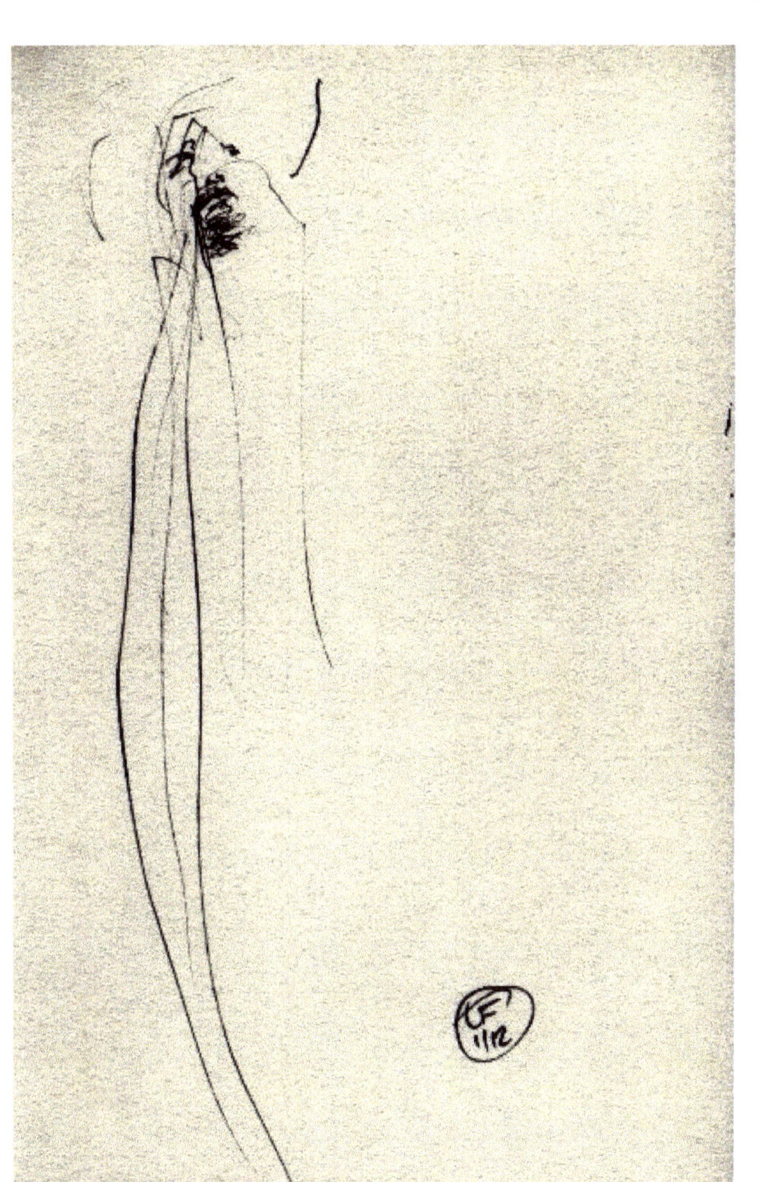

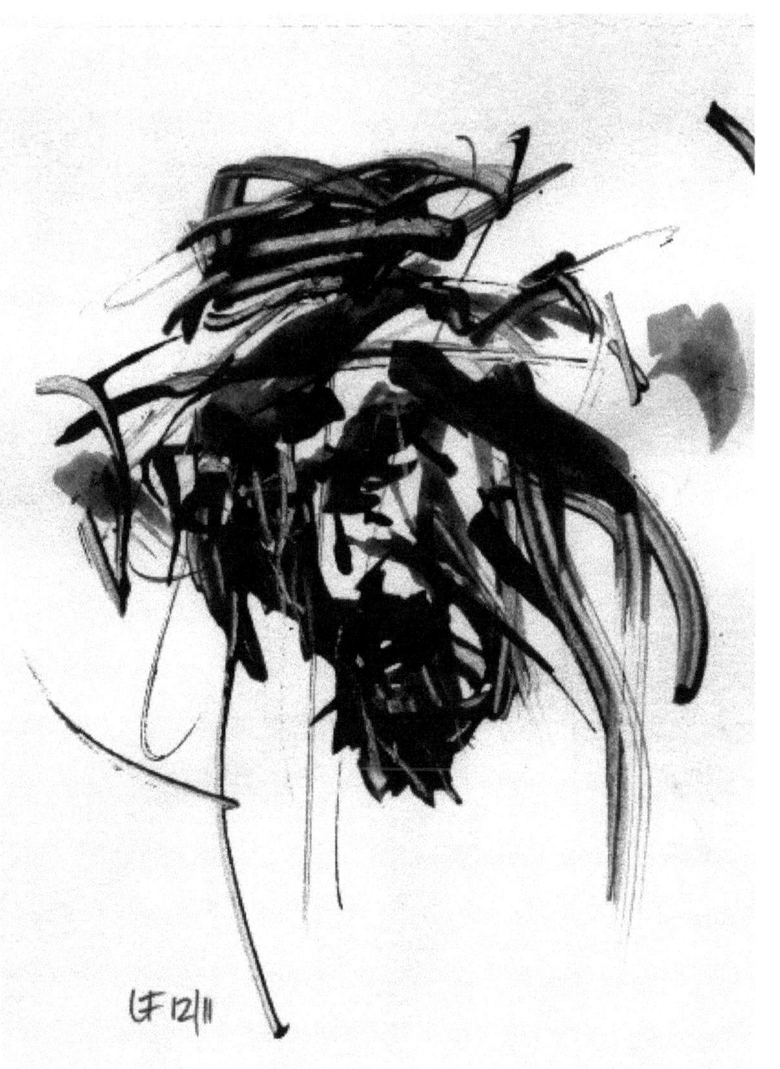
LF 12/11

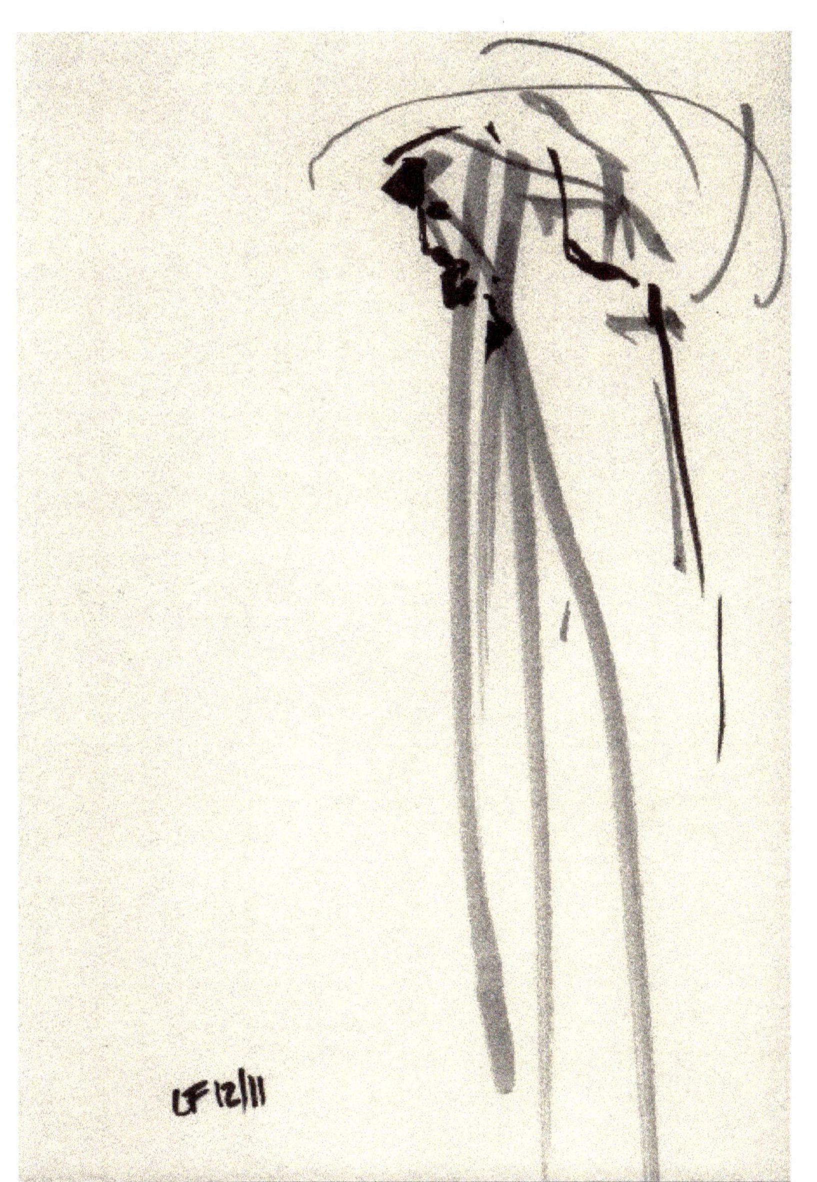
LF 12/11

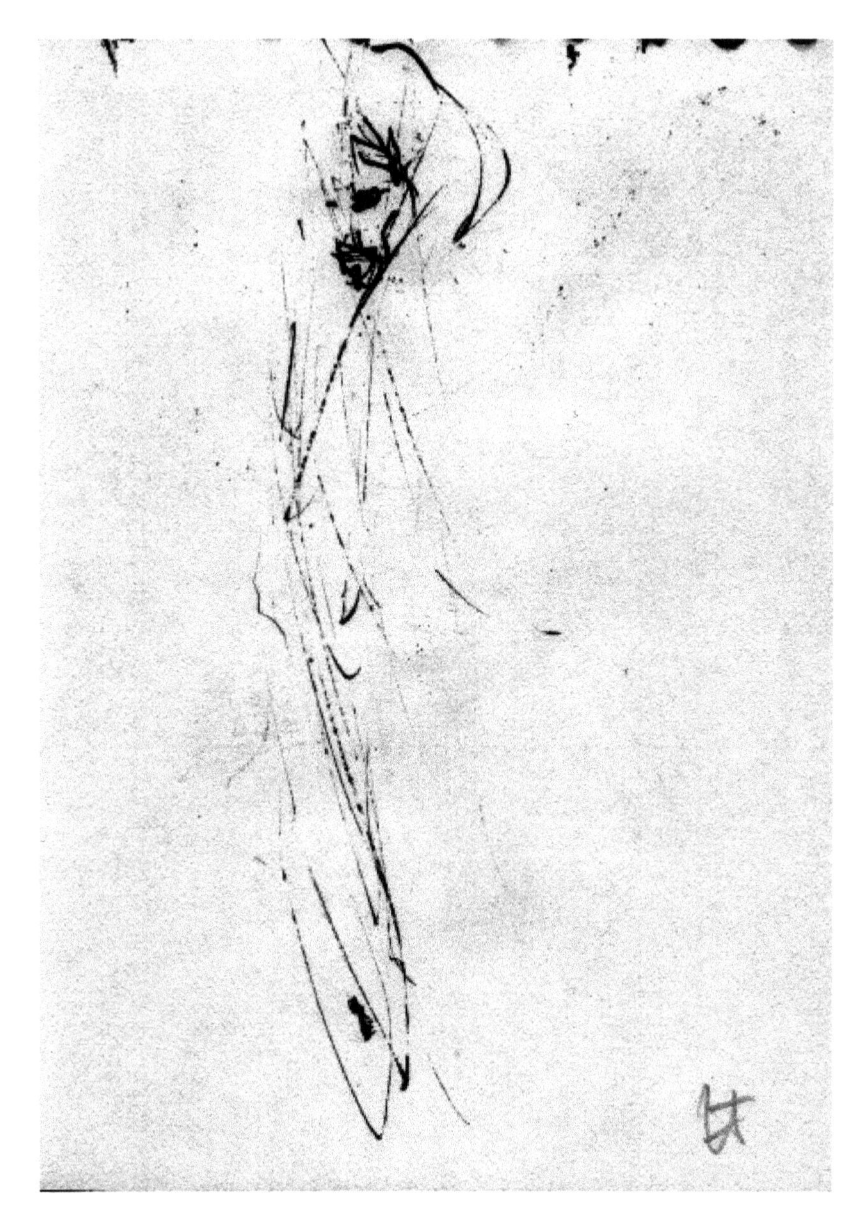

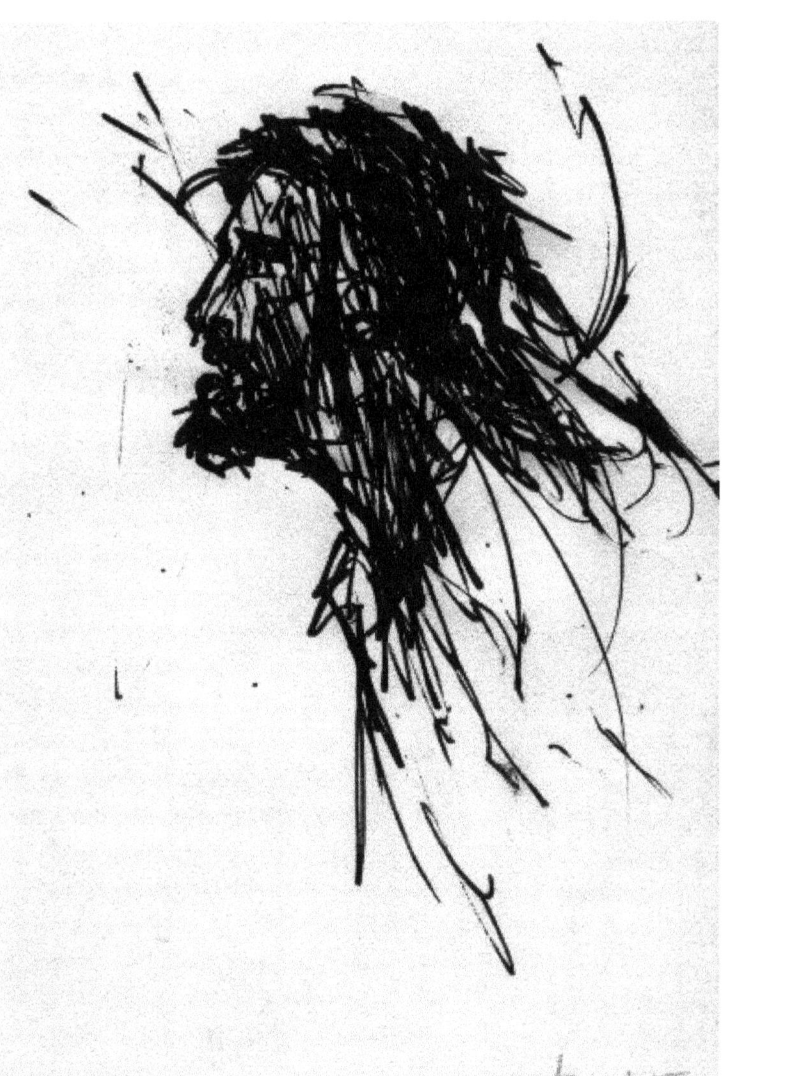

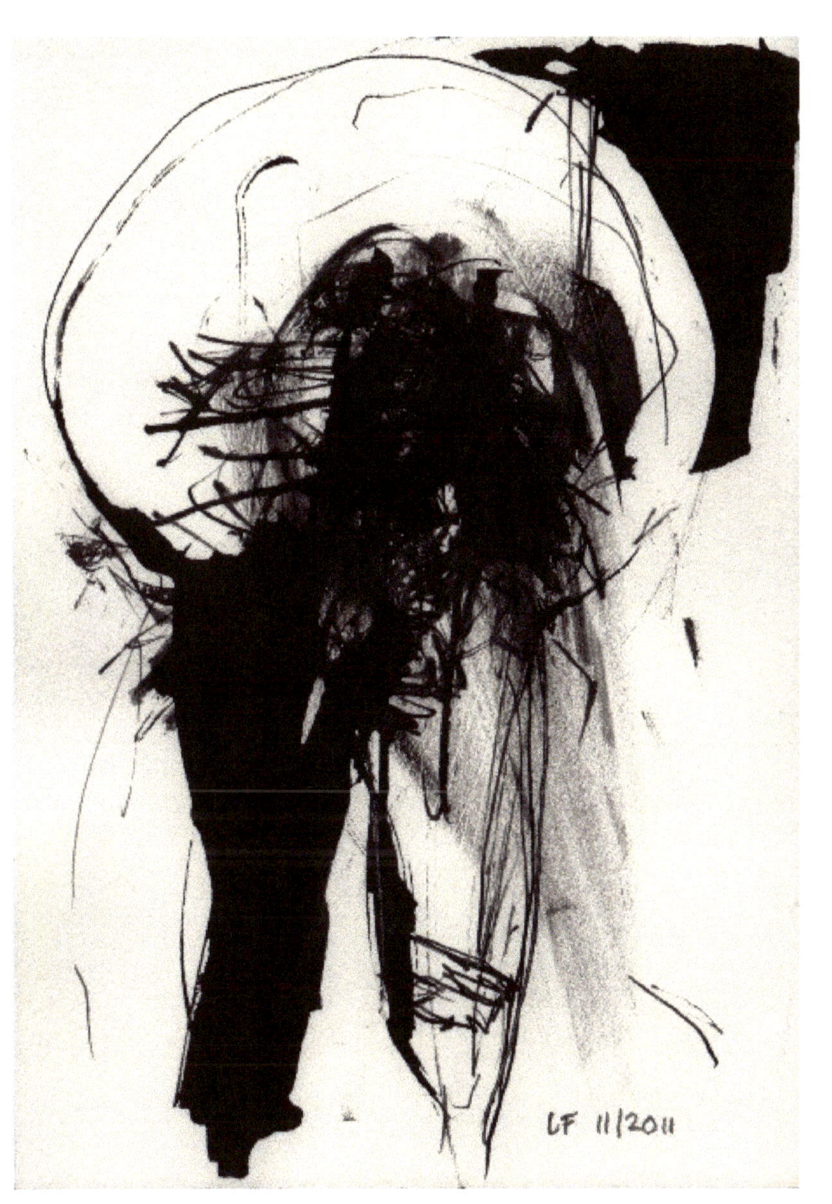
LF 11/2011

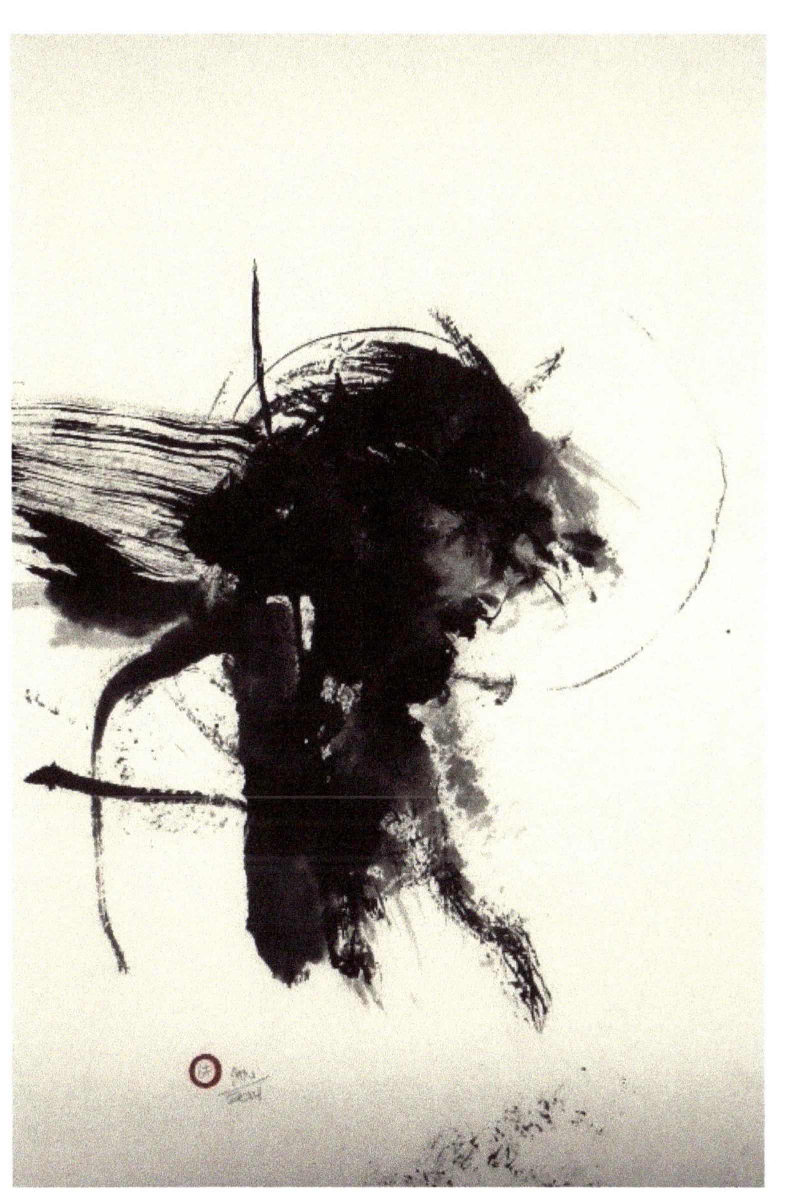

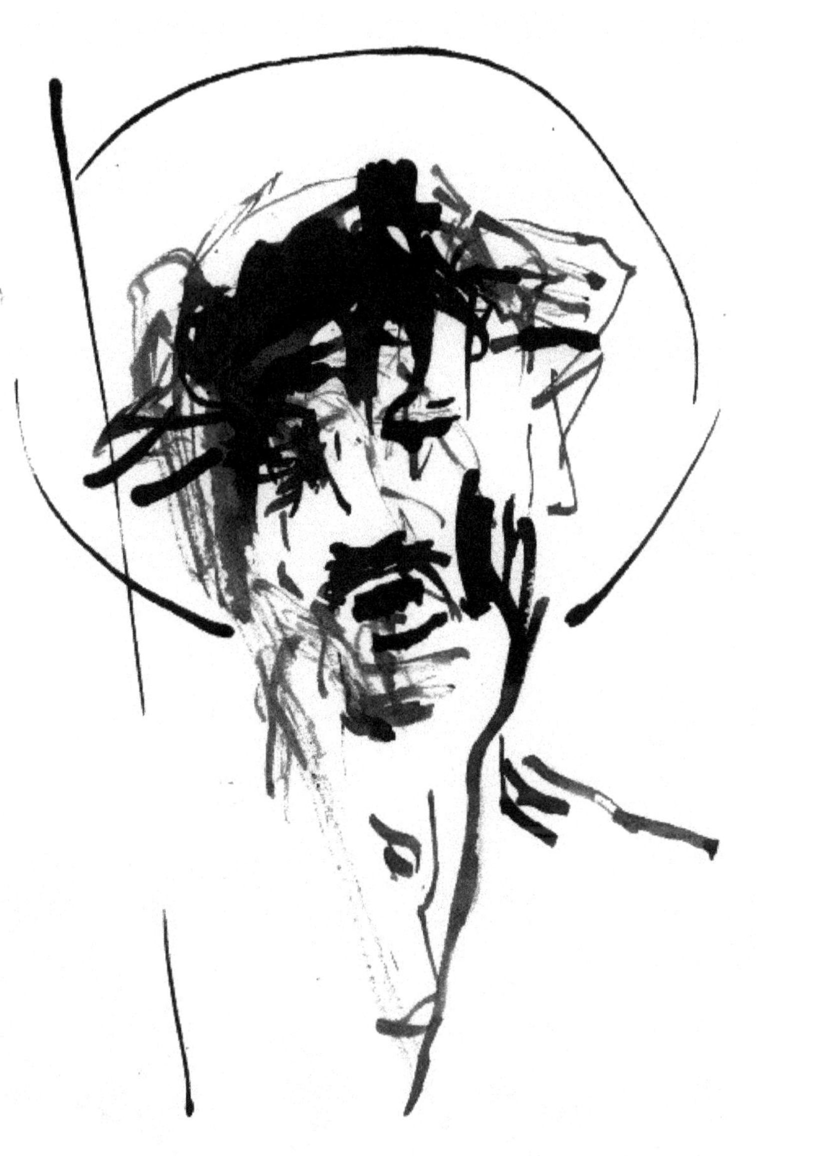

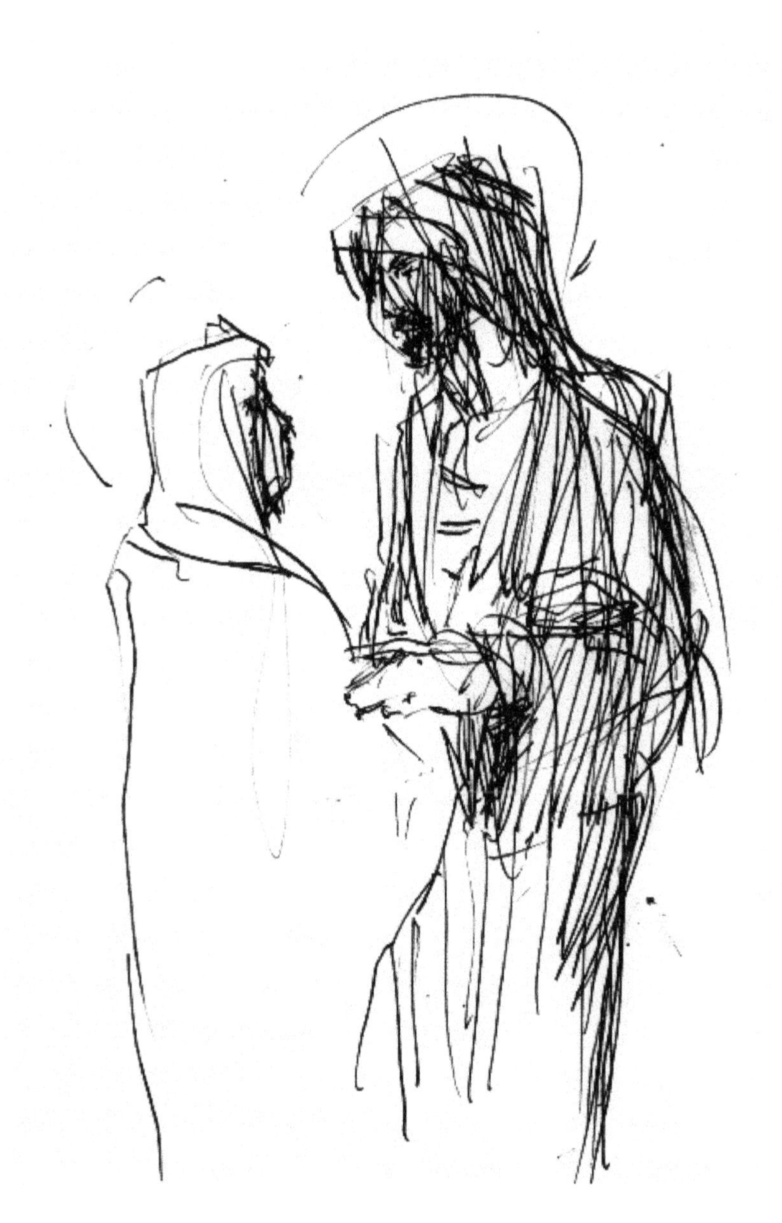

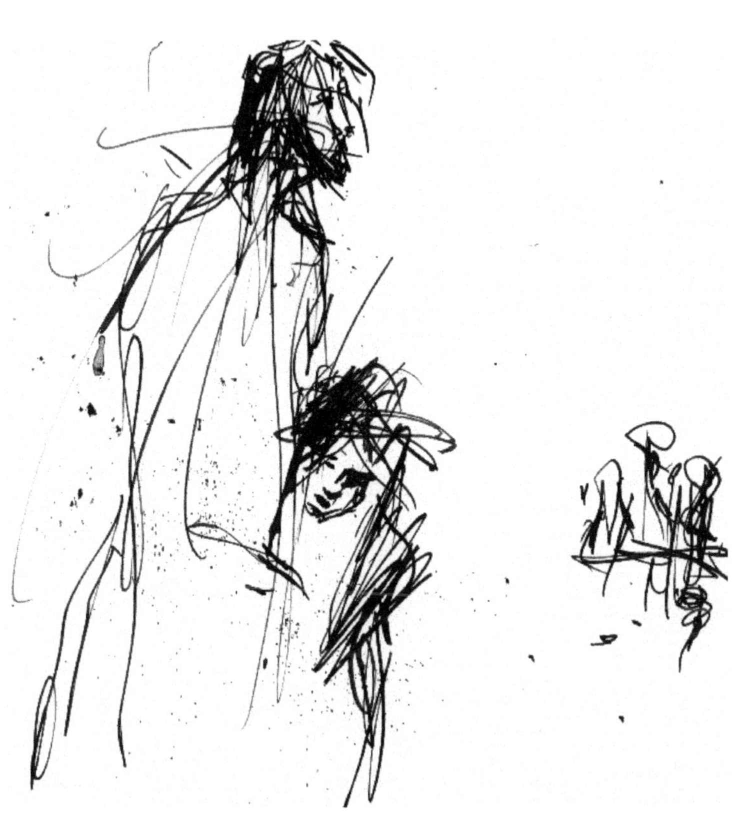

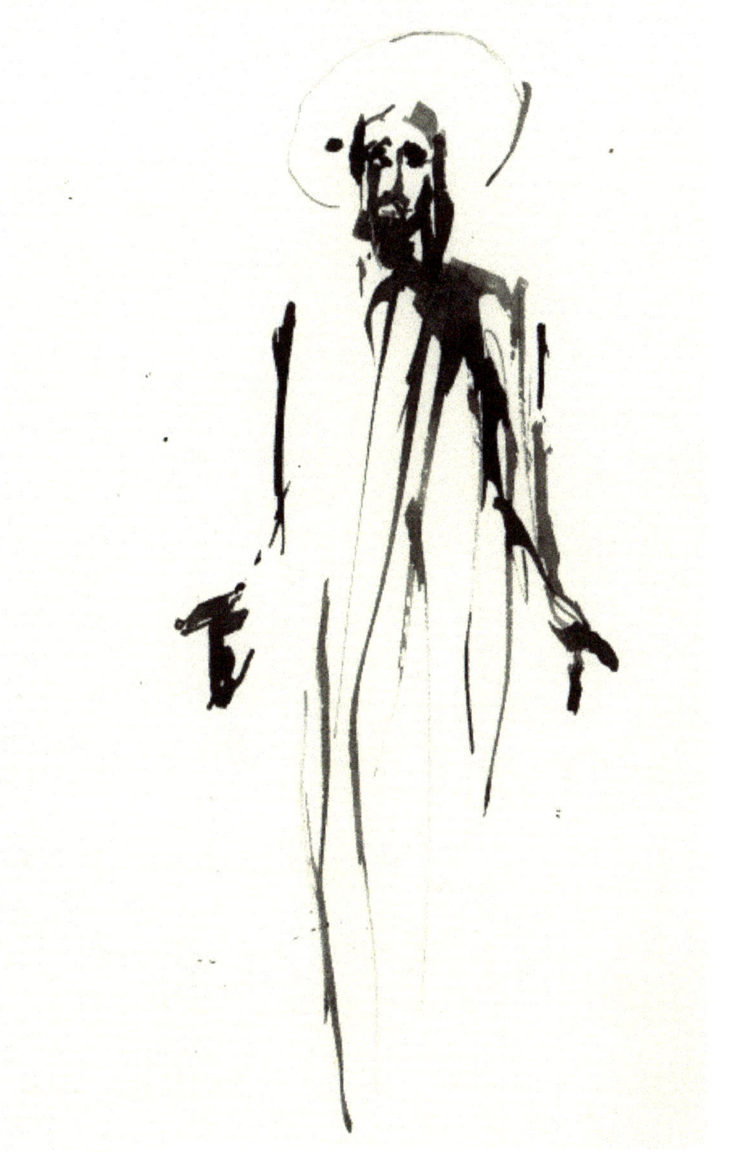

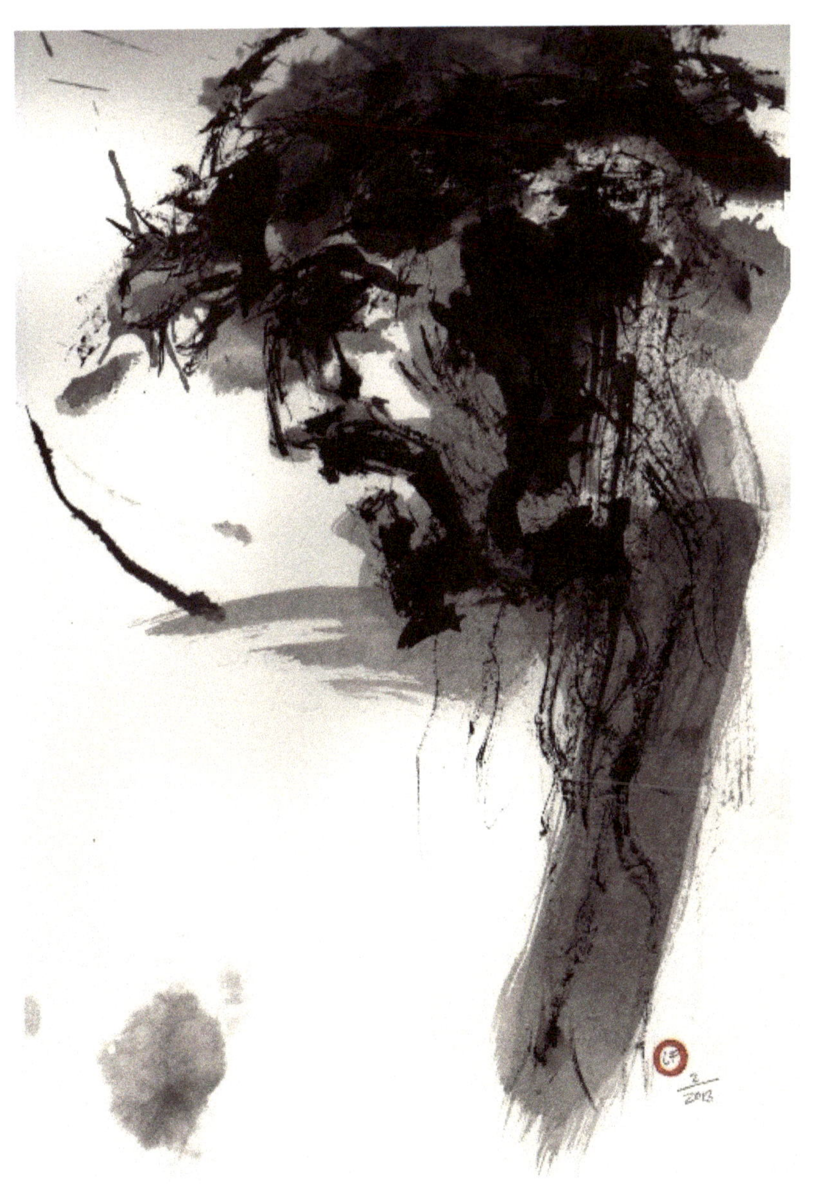

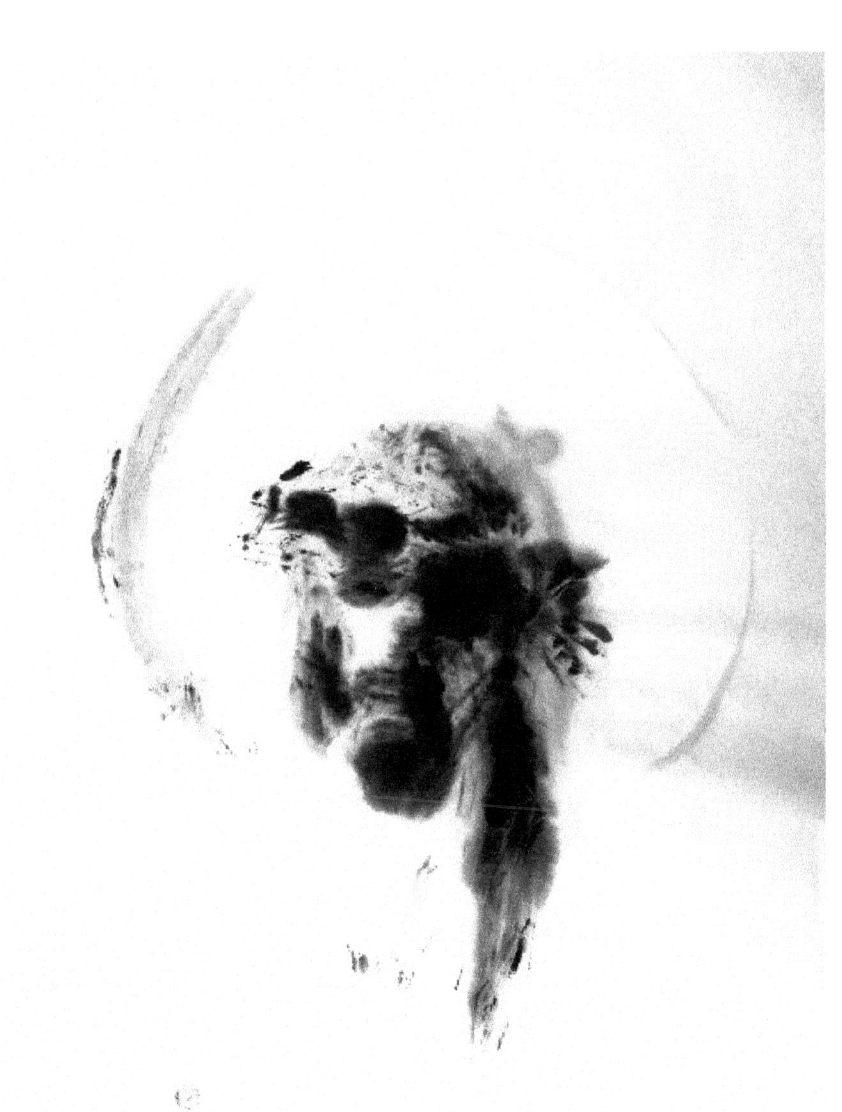

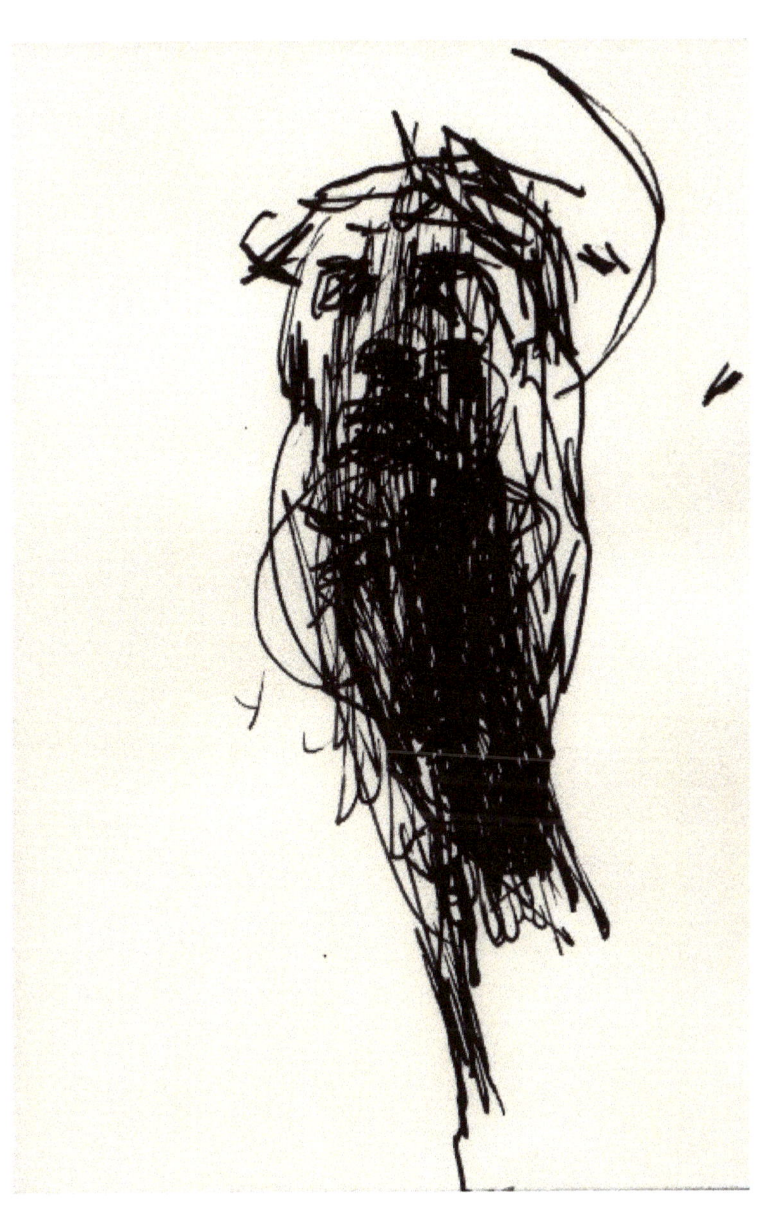

Luc Freymanc

www.freymanc.com